What Have You Lost/Found?

An Anthology of Poetry
Edited by
Dr. Nuzzo-Morgan

International Standard Book Number:

978-1-7947-5623-6

Manufactured in the United States of America

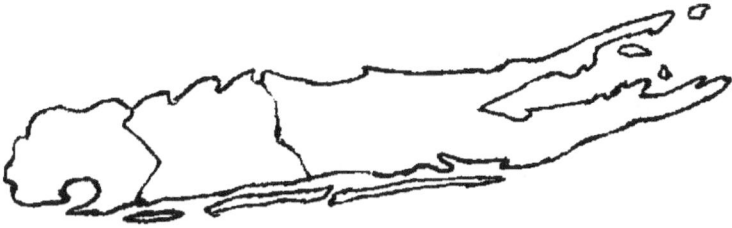

The North Sea Poetry Scene Press
1650 Sycamore Drive
Bohemia, New York 11716

Editor's Note:

Being a newly minted Ph.D., with my dissertation being: The Healing Power of Poetry, now is the right time to publish this project.

I have collected poems from a wide range of poets with a vast range of voices. We have all lost, and/or found, in our lives. This phenomenon is nothing new.

I believe this collection increases the knowledge base of poetry as healer. It offers an opportunity to consider the unique unfolding of loss and/or gain and examine the fullness of personal experience.

Jack Leedy and Gregory Orr have a shared belief in the natural, low-tech healing power of people connecting. The personal lyric narrative was employed in all these poems.

The confessional nature of the poems in *What Have You Lost/Found* is essential for comprehension by the reader, as it "removes the mask" that M.L. Rosenthal wrote about concerning Robert Lowell's book of poems, Life Studies (An Introduction to Confessional Poetry).

My hope is that this collection will create connections, lessen isolation, and assist in developing empathy for our follow humans.

Love, Peace & Poetry!

Dr. Tammy Nuzzo-Morgan

FOREWORD:

Who among us is not encumbered by loss, by the pain of doing without something or someone that once brought us strength, beauty, harmony, meaning? To be human is to love; it is also to survive the loss of what has been dear to us. This is a collection profoundly celebrating what it is to be human. Here, 67 poets search their beings for ways to give voice to some of what has defined them — both in its gift, and in its being taken away. The losses they explore are many; in the first twenty-five pages of poems, we encounter the loss of a childhood home, of mother, of geography, of intimacy and communal experience, of symbols of the self and favorite principles, as well as losses born of drug abuse, aging, fire, and genocide.

But the gravity of the subject is balanced by the gifts discovered — the balm of nature, the music of symphonies, the delight of blueberries and fresh baked bread, the appearance of a singular bird, the glory of the ocean, the patter of pine needles, the bloom of memory, and of pansies. As readers, we are invited to be sustained by the earth itself, by the smell of sand, to be reborn under a new sky.

These are poignant poems, sometimes plaintive personal tales calling as if from an echo chamber, and sometimes cautionary tales heralding the potential of thunderous loss -- the overheating of the earth, the risk of nuclear war. As the collection unfolds, more losses hammer home their significance — betrayal, sexual abuse, suicide, the ravages of alcohol, of a mass shooting. We are called to mourn an unborn child, the change of life, a sister, the loss of a cherished communion dress, a pet hamster. Again, the poets' gifts continue to offer their relief — laughter, psalms, black leather jackets, a grandfather, favorite rocks, the offering of art, of the future, each second alive and well as we notice life around us.

Relying primarily on free verse, only occasionally delving into formal structures in their craft, these poets sing with determined voices. One can dive into the text anywhere; a random opening will yield the invitation of vibrant language as well as the potential comfort of shared experience. I found myself enchanted with key lines and phrases – "Jilted lovers learn to burn/their sorrows into raptures" (David B. Axelrod); "Mother chose duty over divorce" (Leslie Brooke Bell); "stubborn as a bent nail" (David Cain); "Those crows/ will unzip the sky" (Adriana DiGennaro); "in a forest of/ fallen songs" (Kathaleen Donnelly); "your picture hides the 4X12 inch black/ box that holds your ashes" (Peter V. Dugan); "You are ... my metal detector/ as I scour dunes for broken runes of you (George Guida).

Or consider these: "Words...Weighted as apples/On a tree (Peter Thabit Jones); "Fighting with angels/ is a losing proposition" (Norbert Krapf); "a mannequin of a dad" (Maria Lisella); and "my words can cut the spidery threads/ tangled in her memory" (Muriel Harris Weinstein.) This is a brief sampling. I invite you to locate your own favorites. The titles of these poems themselves could ignite a fresh poem of your own making. Scan the CONTENTS pages. Where does your finger rest, your heart stop? Follow this lead. Find your way to the magic of a healing poem, waiting inside you, just below the silence.

November 1, 2021
Carol Barrett, Ph.D.
Professor, Union Institute & University
Author: *Calling in the Bones; Drawing Lessons; Pansies*

Contents

BITTER SELF-AFFLICTION

a second cousin twice removed
nods off within her maxwell house *Haggadah*
between the four questions
and the ten plagues

there's *her* backstory —
snowboarding accident
fractured pelvis painkiller abuse
manipulative skel boyfriend
bank account withdrawals detox withdrawal
father's anguish mother's heartbreak

and tonight —
her pinprick pupils
her sojourns to the bathroom
her slurred *boy-i'm-so-tired* excuses
her coming self-destruction
as together we read passover's backstory
of slavery and freedom

we're afraid for her
fearing the damning prognosis
that she might not survive
the self-imposed shackles
of her own oppression

LOSING CONTROL LITTLE BY LITTLE

we've been opening brokerage accounts
transferring in all of our stocks
i'll no longer have to keep track
of dividends base prices reinvestments

we've found a roofing company
they clean out our gutters
i'll no longer have to maneuver
our 36-foot extension ladder
to scrape out wet leaves with freezing fingers
on frigid december days

my wife had contracted
to have an in-ground sprinkling system installed
i'll no longer have to spend
an hour or two every second or third day
watering the flower beds by hand
positioning sprinklers every thirty minutes
on our front and back lawns

as much as i've enjoyed the responsibility
of keeping spreadsheets of our investments
climbing up the ladder
standing with a pistol grip nozzle
i'm told it's good to let someone else do it for now

it's been difficult giving up these obligations
these encumbrances
these duties
which make me feel alive
and needed

LOSS NOT FOUND

unrepentant ghosts of sorrow
scratching tell-tale souvenirs
into facial fault lines
a living canvas taut with grief

unshed memories today tomorrow
fragility fueled by ever-fears
behind a mask a haunted smile
searching yearning no relief

NEVER DISCARDED

> hey look, I found a letter
     she unfolded a yellowed loose-leaf sheet
     filled with dark angry scrawls
> it's one I wrote to you back in eighty-two
> you know when things between us weren't so good

I acknowledged her discovery with a grunt
     though blurred some by decades
     i'll never forget those harsh nights
     of hurt accusations and discord

< you want me to read it?
     I reached out my hand
< or is it another of those letters you wrote only for
yourself?

> no, not really
     answered only the first of the two questions
> anyway it's missing page two
     as she re-folded it and slipped it away

didn't want to watch where it went
     probably in the kitchen cabinet
     behind the aspirin and the vitamin c

wondered why she hadn't torn it to shreds
     or burned it back then
     when she was yearning for a serenity
     I couldn't provide

SEARCHING FOR CATHARSIS

I was halfway out
on my north-south walking loop
listenin' to israeli jazz on my mp3
while percolatin' and cogitatin' about
an idea-seed for a poem

and I couldn't latch onto
a certain word –
a certain *goddamn* word
that I knew meant
the release of repressed emotions

I got close several times
sometimes it was just within reach ...
synchronization popped into mind
and *catheterization*
though I hadn't realized until after
how close *catheter* actually was

I knew ... or at least *hoped*
that the word would eventually come ...
I hate being held captive
by my own mental decrepitude
accompanied by the fear
– always that horrible unnameable fear –
that I was ... you know ...
losin' it

Richard L. Adinolfi

ODE TO JAMESPORT BAY

Oh bay of Jamesport,
what transport of delight
in your transcendent presence
to divine depths of the soul
nowhere else delivers.

Specs of light dance "tap"
upon ripples of tranquil waters
of sunlit blue,
that extend to low lying contours
of peninsula grounded bright
with tree greens
in an outline of sandy beige shores
with the faint view of a home or two.

Where under an ephemeral expanse
of powder blue skies brushed
with hovering faint white clouds,
a seagull flaps her outstretched wings
and soars on high in flight
across the boundless reaches
of eternity's balm.

While footsteps impress the soft moist sand
beneath strolling feet,
a pale rainbow
of tiny smooth stones and white shells
color patted furrows of light tan sand,
when I turn to face the opposite terrain

and view the bay in all its plenitude
of blue, white, green and tan too,
and hear the foamy waters
swish near below
and raise my hands in prayer
to poise in reverence there to you.

Sharon Anderson

AMONG THE FALLEN

When I was small
I danced among the leaves
weaving in spirals
of unchecked joy
chasing a dream

When I was young
I gathered fallen leaves
tossed them aloft
in a spin of delight
feeding a dream

As I grew old
I sprawled among the leaves
feeling them wither
along my spine
leaching my dreams

And now as I repine
I hold a single leaf
follow the veined design
and ache to know
if ever it held a dream

Raymond Philip Asaph

WHERE FIRE WAS

Though we've walked all day
down soft brown paths
cooled by the shade
of still-living trees,
this place where fire was—
the blackened ground,
the smoke-scented stones,
and the blue hole
in the green canopy—seems now
the truest part of the woods
until, bright red on a scorched branch,
one
cardinal
sings.

MORE

When you took off your clothes
in my apartment and dropped them on the floor,
I wanted to be more
than one more of your lovers. I wanted to go
into the dreams with you,
make you laugh in the morning, make you wait
for breakfast, take you to the park
at the heart of town, point out the gestures
of children and show you how close
love is to us. I was going to crush the buds
of lavender for you, hold my hands under your nose
and tell you to breathe. When I found the sea
and rode your waves, when I pulled your hair
and pounded you with pleasure,
I wanted to be more than an evening's ecstasy,
more than fun in the form of a man.
I was going to eat a bowl
of blueberries with you, kiss your stained lips,
show you my favorite scriptures,
share the passages that shaped my life,
give you the gifts that were given me.
I wanted you to close your eyes with me
and listen to the whole sixth symphony.
And I wanted to hear you sing.
When I caressed your face
with my fingertips, I thought you knew this,
and I believed you knew you were holding an ocean
when you held my shoulders.

But you did not enter any of my mansions,
saw none of the flowers
I scattered in my mind at your feet.
You picked up your clothes and put them on again
and left me drenched with your scent, an instrument
echoing with your sensations.

LOST IN THE LANDSCAPE

In the face of a great horizon,
I dissolve.
All of my grand plans,
my ceaseless worries,
and my nagging thoughts
disperse into the atmosphere
like carbonation rising from an open soda can.

For the moment,
I feel the pressure release-
the pressure of being me.
I am no longer my name,
my history,
or this pair of eyes suspended behind a bag of skin,
constantly judging and projecting fear onto the world around
me.
I just *am*.

I am the wind
the mountains
and the nebulous clouds.
My eyes bathe in the sun
and my lungs drink in the trees.
My nerves reach outward like branches to touch the horizon
while my toes root into the earth.
I am no longer a lonely raindrop lost at sea,
I am the ocean.

David B. Axelrod

AFTER I CAUGHT MY GIRLFRIEND

After I caught my girlfriend
in bed with another man—
worse, a fellow writer whose
talent made me jealous—
I took to my car and drove
two hundred miles in no
direction. The engine did
not overheat or fume. Only
I emitted odorous epitaphs
and curses no catalytic
converter could capture.
Jilted lovers learn to burn
their sorrows into raptures.

BLACK MOUNTAIN

Legend met poetry in the Black
Mountains. Creeley, Duncan, Olsen—
a gaggle of poets, a bagel of Beats
all camping in Reviews. I drove
to the Blue Ridge, early spring,
wending narrow roads in North
Carolina to the town called Black
Mountain where nothing looked
beat except Main Street. "Welcome
to Black Mountain, Home of Longest
Fairway in America," said the billboard
over a gas station. If I imagined
poets musing in the Five and Dime—
I found only wincing clerks, wondering
about a stranger. Another thirty
miles of narrow mountain road took me
to a gate locked across the passage:
"Closed for Winter. Danger, Icy Roads."
The mist of spring rose from retreating
snow banks. A startling sun gleamed
off my orange Super Beetle. I rubbed
my scraggly beard, turned around
and drove back through Black
Mountain, reviewing where history
meets legend and how I thought
this town was where it happened.

BLIND, DEAF AND DUMB

Romantic love
lays siege to reason

      They tell us
       love is blind.

making summer
of any season.

      Must we be deaf
      and dumb besides?

CLOROX

The most effective mix is
ten to one to kill whatever germs.
Still, in the spirit of overdosing,
I pour it straight from the bottle
onto the floor. I've learned to
not wear clothes I value. Alone,
I might wear only underwear,
spreading the liquid with a rag
as my eyes tear. I've burned off
my fingerprints, bleached my
knees and soles. Lungs scorched,
I cough as I cry for all my blemishes.

THE DEATH OF AMERICAN POETRY

came slowly as help for an indigent on a waiting-room chair
waiting to be seen in an emergency room promising patients'
rights where a medical clerk sure on first sight of no
insurance cued an orderly who denied a stretcher let alone a
blanket. The analogies had worn so thin—no longer any
metaphors—and of course no meaning. Pity was a cliché and
empathy inconsiderable. So, this young woman intern who,
herself, had a hundred reasons to care, chose instead to only
glance once, allowing the others—white men, Americans, 6'
or taller, Christian mostly and duly credentialed—to engage
in collegial chatter, sneaking over just once to stare into the
fixed and dilated pupils confirming in their reflection the
murderer whose image at least was clearly captured if only
in dead eyes.

Sybil Bank

I CANNOT FIND

the turtle dove
perched among
smoky green pines
as it pumps its chest
cracks the dawn with soaring trill.

I cannot smell

the early morning scent of
heavy sticky cones dropping
onto slippery jumbles
of pine needles.

I cannot see

clouds rise
to unsheathe the mountain
where wild blue rock
patterns threads of copper.

I cannot touch

fuchsia heath pushing between crevices
painting color and shadow
playing with the wind in
my childhood home

but my soul remembers
pauses in many landscapes
where tense trees bend toward the sea
where wine lands purple the tawny light
where white washed houses call.

Yes

There is Africa

SWEDASAI – LITHUANIA – 2004

a bone thin horse struggles through mud
squat monotonous houses huddle
bent women trudge with bundles of kindling
gray-bearded men smoke on corners
the young have left

chill wind skims through tangled root and shrub
mass graves of those who screamed hopeless prayers
limp sun tires and dips
morbid sky gives up on light
the lost past given to you like pieces of mosaic
further away a stone courtyard
bricks like newly baked loaves
set in a splendid archway where
serene angels fill golden cornices
old women in thick stockings rake leaves
plant pansies where
upright gravestones
show names forever inscribed

my aunt once lived here
I show the women her photograph
they shake their heads
point to the mass graves
"Judah," one says

some bones are anonymous

TRANSITIONS – 1986

A Triptych

1. The Night their Mother Dies

Her brother calls –
"The old lady is gone," he says.

Television at the airport brays its news.
The Challenger Space Shuttle slowly dissolves,
surreal orangey plumes of fire
dip the fractured carcass into icy seas.

Graves of ocean, earth and fire roam her mind.
Blood red African sun blazes through the airplane
windows
pockets of light shudder molten flicks of silver.
Below the immensity of this country, land of
grass, desert, mountain, lushness and poverty.

The plane descends,
sweeps its shadow across brown scrub
airport shimmers its glass windows
dares the eye to resist the glare.
With the toe of her shoe she
scratches off a patch of earth
the smell of dry sweet sand, the clay undertow
the wild yellow summer flowers, delicately drooping
their angled heads make her dizzy – she picks just
one.

2. Earth to Earth

She wakes to clear blue, white light,
the mountain named for a crouching lion, hovers,
sweeps its shadow across the brown scrub that
nests its haunches.

She had thought that at the graveside
she would scratch off a patch of earth
with her shoe
hoist a shovel and cover a plain wooden box
with that dry, sweet sand, the clay undertow.

But
her mother left instructions for cremation,
ashes to be scattered.
Like a train going nowhere on silent wheels
the coffin slides into fire.
The immensity of this country, land of
grass, desert, mountain, lushness and poverty,
now owns a daughter's sorrow – dust to dust.

Grey-white grit rises, as what was her mother
flies back in the churlish wind.
The earth resists,
it does not blend – but it will.
It will quietly take these ashes into its heart,
its heart of dry, sweet sand, the clay undertow.

3. Africa's Heated Heart

is left behind.
The other part of her will reside
far from the vastness of its grass, desert,
lushness and poverty.
She scratches off a piece of earth with her shoe
the remembered dry, sweet sand, its clay undertow.

Flying the high skies of the north
she looks down
at alps, plains, lakes
swept with unsmutched snow.

In the icy stretches of Europe
or the huge arc of America
she continues her life

knows its blemishes, its loss –
Comes out from under the sweep of shadow
finds her piece of earth.

CPR

A heart no longer
       Broken
       Blackened
       Scarred

       Lost

Love slowly drained
       No Hope
       No Feeling
       No Pain

       Nothing

Atrophied through neglect
Tossed on the scrap heap of love

There you found me
Something worth salvaging
Delicate restoration
       Faith
       Hope
       Love6

       Patience

Infused life
      Stronger
      Healthier
      Happier

      Alive

Love reborn
      By you
      For you
      With you

Amy Barone

DEAD FOX

The devil winked and she erupted
into petty remarks, my trusted

colleague whose nasty looks I viewed
from hidden eyes. She sabotaged my work,

falsely vented to bosses.
Betrayal comes in shades of violet,

so I wore orange and blue to deflect
malice and envy. I lost sisters to greed,

so I can handle strangers.
Slaying the fox now comes easy.

PICKING UP THE PIECES

Nearly everything I drop in my tiny abode shatters.
A bathing suit's thick pink strap holder cracked
in half when it hit the wood floor.

Thinking of an annoying friend, I dropped the lid
to my Fortnum & Mason sugar jar. It served me
twenty years, outliving the friendship with the gift giver.

Bent on celebrating every day, I drink from my late
mother's crystal glasses while they last. Every few months,
a long stem falls away from a thick chalice when it meets

the hard granite counter. Never a clean break.
During dusting, the lid of a valuable Rose Medallion
candy jar slips from my hand. A clean break. Sweet.
Inspired, I resolve to embrace joy when I dust, drink,
think.

SHAPESHIFTER SISTER

Once cloaked in a red cape,
she eventually changed stylists.

Never claimed her own thoughts.
Chose interests by boyfriend—

dated golf and champagne.
Married ice hockey and beer.

Dreamed big, worked little.
Career took a backseat to kids.

Can't manage time or money.
My late mother functioned as her bank ATM.

She wants another loan, plus my freedom.
Now, who's the wolf?

UNFINISHED

At dusk, small penguins wash ashore at Phillip Island.
They hesitate, waddle forward, swish backwards

into the surf, not ready to embrace the night.
We stopped speaking, if you can call words

sent to a computer screen, on a random basis, talk.
You hide like the little animals burrowing in the sand,

free from strangers' stares and forbidden camera flashes.
I spoke to my last lover by phone. Lured him with voice.

Sound incited hearts. Words weren't shackled to a screen.
Playful, they flew on waves, bouncing from soul to soul.

Carol Barrett

HOME MOVIE

I'm in diapers,
nonchalant,
when your small

hands approach
with a white bonnet,
struggle to fit it

to my head. Triumph:
my face half hidden.
I never realized

what I took
from you – your small
life, your small room

split in two.
My world *joined,*
always another voice

in the dark
where breathing merges,
morning light

never wakes alone.
That day on the beach
you did not

return, Daddy drove
over oceans
of sand, searching

for your twelve-year-old
body in the dunes,
instructing me

not to look
on shore, but
in the waves.

I knew you were out
beyond all agony.
He turned back

to base, Mother
holding her breath
in a labor

outside time. *Call
the authorities* he said.
But I knew

you had walked
all the way to the last
pier. You watched gulls

gulping on long
dives, your lungs
filling

with something
like silence.
You didn't go

far enough I insisted.
And because
there was nothing

else to do,
Daddy took the truck
back out, spinning

the quiet of a man
who hopes in the long dusk
that the child

beside him
might have a chance
of being right.

Farther, I said,
Farther.
It was you:

that slip of wind
and hair
a stone's throw

from the pier.
This pairing of
purpose has become

second nature.
Once,
all my life

I slept in the same
room with you. Nothing
changes that.

IMPELLED TOWARD LIGHT

I carried only the weight of my mother's
instruction: get a good tree.
My father's hatchet strapped to his belt,
Lady's ears perked for the gambit,
we crossed the highway and skittered
rocks on the old logger's run
to Beaver Dam. Storm timbers
catapulted over the road, still greening:
some we ducked and some we straddled,
the pitch gumming our senses, the path now
a grassy funnel. I tagged spruce,
then pine, height and girth weighed out
in the echoing gorge: poor match
for the fullness of my father's vision.

The year before, my mother disenchanted
with his lean choice, he drilled holes
in the trunk, stuffed boughs to fill
the bare space. Grafted branches don't bend
with the grace of native;
the want in his gift stuck out
in all directions. This year:
a noble fir, grown deep under the forest
roof, its young trunk made to seek the light
slowly, not in quick summer spurts
sprawling skyward. He was after
a burly prize, thick with competition.

So we took to the brush,
salmon berry and bramble, boulders

and lightning-split stumps sprouting ferns,
scalloped fungus. I followed my father's
lead as if trained on it, tree to tree
on the steep bank, heady with exuberance,
the prick of Oregon grape.

Not knowing where we were, I figured
the oozing gullies to lead dam-ward
somewhere below. My father's compass
fixed on another pole: my mother's pleasure.
Knees to the slope, humus sliding
over red clay, I reveled in keeping up,
knew the light was leaving, certain
of the gauge: his hand on the horizon.
Soaked in tiredness, I pulled up
on the nearest flounce, wondered
how we'd haul it, back over the wild,
the wake of tripped blackberry.

Still in pursuit, his hair whickered
with needles, suddenly my father understood
Lady was not with us. He assumed
the child would know the dog's
boundings, furry troop on our flank.
I assumed he knew what mattered:
where the beaver live, where the best
trees grow, where we were, all of us.
In that moment, more than Lady was lost.

There is a shade of darkness they call
pitch black, and in that shade
we came finally to the house,

hatchet still unsheathed.
He carried her wet wool form
all the way back, angling up the cliff,
deciding dark would beat us
on the old road. I grew up hearing
when lost on a mountain, follow
a stream out. Here, that saving
principle in reverse, working
but without precision: to climb
at night is to crawl.

First light, my mother's face:
the same frozen agony, that day
my sister disappeared on Klipsan Beach
headed for the lighthouse.
My father ran fresh water for Lady, left
me to explain, all that time, no tree.

Years later I took my first lover
down the road to Beaver Dam.
The freedom of live cover
alluring, he undressed me
in splotchy sunlight, layers
peeling back like damp leaves,
my hands curling to his mouth
like trilliums on a mossy bed,
his heat flush with the sky.

Despite that woodsy sheet of honeysuckle
air, the chorus of chickadees, the earth
warm as stones in an open stream,
I could not remove the strain

of my father's shoulders hugging the cliff,
Lady panting in his arms, my own
small feet worrying their way upward,
new with knowing he had misjudged
the world, or I, his aim.

I look for the beaver now,
their gray wash of work. Interlocking
vines stifle the path, a small voice
squeezed to unending silence, the late
October berries dark with juice,
my father's first failure
smarting in my hand.

LARKSPUR TRAIL

As is their habit, they lunch Tuesday
at the Senior Center, save the saltines
for later, inquire after Berta, and Jim.

Pine boughs nod their whisking yes
to this noble exercise of heart
and song, this wind-swept walk along

a foaming creek that pulls north
like a drunken river, the walkers' arms
latched to torsos, ambling in rhythm,

hands hooked in loose seam, heads
cocked to the rush of water over wet
slate. A child in plaid skirt skips ahead

like a small stone tossed from the wrist.
A spaniel heads their way, bounding
beyond his master, pulling, intent

on covering the sun-smoked turf
before the sky can shift gears, settle
the doves in rafters, the quail in coveys

among the sage. The dog is happy
as the smell of barbecues
drifts through cedar slats. He makes

the walkers' faces light. When they began,
they did not know any of this:
girl, dog, bird, pine, stream. Only

that the body needs its ground,
its holy place in the fine dust of things.
Nuthatch nesting, they won't tell where.

CAPE COD BARRACKS

We were good girls
when he carried our mother
across the threshold of
her cozy cape cod home.

Dragged up by inept parents
and hardened at eighteen
in the jungles of World War II,
he declared us sneaky little girls
ruined by his I bride,
and found us all in need
of a stronger authority.

The honeymoon over,
his campaign to reorder
our lives began,
while joy and laughter
died of bewilderment
in the cape cod barracks.

The kitchen became a mess hall
where plates were picked clean in silence.
Homework was inspected nightly,
hair and hemlines every morning,
offenders confined to their rooms,
Mother ignored with weeks of silence
if she dared to intervene.

Our dead father's relatives were banished,
family friends rudely dismissed.
Neighbors stayed away.
The front door was guarded against
juvenile sex fiends,
and entry denied to anyone with
peace signs or hippie hair.

Little sister AWOL'd at seventeen.
Mother chose duty over divorce.
I walked the perimeters of their marriage,
until the death of that unlovable man
who never had a childhood
and nearly killed mine.

HOT STUFF

I was hotter than hot at twenty-one,
drowning men in pheromones.

Still hot at thirty-one,
I was strutting the high wire
of exquisite sexual tension.

Sensuality,
my elixir of youth
at forty-one,
looking thirty.

Fifty-one.
Feeling hotter than hot,
then colder than cold.
Pheromones
high wire tension
sensual elixir
drowning in menopause.

PSALM

I no longer sing with the radio
while taking the parkway from
one sad destination to another.

These days,
I am the wreck traveling between
the nursing home and the graves,
my screams scattering traffic,
my tears leaving rock salt trails
atop the black macadam.

The only thing saving me from
the break-down lane,
the only solace for my dwindling family
in these saddest of times,
is our version of The Twenty-Third Psalm.

You'll never hear it on the radio,
or from the parkway wreck.
But, if you come to the nursing home
and the graves,
join your hands and voices with ours,
you will find earthly comfort in
flesh pressing flesh,
voices layering harmonies

in praise for the One who leads us
to lush meadows' sustenance,
tranquility by undisturbed waters,
freedom from fear of Death,
and eternal life in celestial peace.

SIPPY CUP

Their young bodies lacking
hand-to-mouth coordination,
toddlers with heart shaped lips,
eagerly slurp from sippy cups

while I, lacking the same,
drink from travel mugs
designed for adults-on-the-go.

I've forsaken china
for these covered mugs,
my lips pursed in perpetual pleats,
taking cautious sips although
I'm only going from the coffee pot
to my kitchen table.

Can't even roam through
a good poetry book
without them, anymore.
Plastic from 7-11,
sassy red aluminum from Starbucks,
cobalt blue mystery-metal from the dollar store,

all meant to distract me from the truth
that my coordination is regressing,
and one day I'll be slurping decaf
out of sippy cups
designed for geriatric mouths and hands.

Maggie Bloomfield

LOSS

I did not take care of you,
young inebriate that I was.
The blooming breasts were
a bit of a thrill,
but your journey
within my womb
caused
the scotch I needed
for survival
to make me nauseous,
angry at the injustice
of consequence.

I had you plucked from me like a grape
and never looked back
till years later
when you're not here
to go shopping,
or house hunting,
or to a hockey game,
or the theatre,
to tell you to get the hair
out of your eyes,
or shine your shoes,
or iron your shirt,
to plead with you to
finish college,
or beg you to move

closer to home.

Peter D. Bové

WHEN I WAS FIVE

What ever became of us?
So long ago it was.
Ran free and slept...
So elusive it was...
'Cept for pin-up girls and stuff...

I plunder, planet-struck through years...

Labor Day Parade...
Where did I go? The times I forgot...
Jelly stain hot spot cloudy day kite.
-- A life and a half in just under a night.
Who knew how grotesque it could be?
Chased by sorrow or fear.

Morning light, and when it's all over
-- The decoder watch and the homemade wine.
The old pumpkin patch...
The first girl's hoots...
Borrow and born now.
Boozin' a little bit.

Rosalind Brenner

APART

At dusk the flashing red lights of police cars
parked near the empty beach
efface the glow of sunset.
Across the way on Ocean Drive
people are watching and being watched.

For so long you have been my comet
and I have clung to your eccentric orbit.
That's why I had to leave, to see if
attending to my own footsteps
I might overcome the pointless
the unimportant, the tired.

But now, here am I,
eyeing others in the light
of their apartment windows,
fixed in this wanderer's sadness
in the quiet of being alone
that pulls apart resolve.
I know goodbye
is permanent and love

a throb of tenderness and all the rest,
so clear in this lonesome interlude,
something else.

ON GARDINER'S BAY

It's winter now and we have left
our kayak on the dock,
hoping, I guess, that though the season
has been rattling the cabin,
we would move the kayak soon,
hoping, the way we tend to hope,
that we could paddle once more
before real weather hit.
You and I are like that.
Our separate busyness, the way we pay
attention to our own small ways
till big waves breach our door.

But now, this storm. We must retrieve
our boat or watch our pleasure
sink in Gardiner's Bay. The way
our pleasure in each other lifts us,
then drifts, then disappears
into the currents of the years.

We press headlong into the wind,
push forward as it pushes us back.
Familiar: the way we do this to each other.
Salty rivulets pour into our squishing boots,
soak our jeans, anoraks.
You lift your hands to your face
as if this gesture will protect you
against flying branches
and the avalanche of foam that slams
the banks above the sea wall.

Blinking to keep our eyes open
we pull our kayak from its rack.
The boat strains at ropes and bungees,
cockpits turn with gusts.
We heave it against the wind,
drag and drop it leeward of the cabin.
reach the seeming safety
of our door, force it open, yank it shut
on its straining hinges.

Lightning streaks jagged flares
into the bay, illuminates the white-out scene.
The jalousies fly, glass shatters
and the timbers creak.
You look like a man
who could climb Everest,
a man possessed.

I say I'm scared. All I feel from you is air.
You say you wouldn't mind dying,
released into a gale,
the wind and you shrieking.
We strip off our dripping clothes,
fall into our old water bed.
You reach across the waves
to hold me.

Richard Bronson

SYNCHRONICITIES
for Wylee

Friends take us to their favorite restaurant,
a crowded Broadway place, and in the buzz
of conversation, engaged in talk of wine and food,
I hear your voice –
a choral singer's unmistakable timbre
not heard for a decade or more.
I turn and it is you, seated at a neighboring table,
in this city of millions!

And two months ago, concerned about a friend
I was unable to reach three days in a row,
we meet next day in *Whole Foods*,
pushing shopping carts down the same isle.

And last year, an unexpected encounter
in a packed gallery. Colleagues who'd crossed the Atlantic
unaware of each other's plans meet at the Tate Modern!

Are we marionettes in some hermetic drama,
the paths we choose illusion, and forces
beyond the limits of our minds at work?

David Cain

NET RAP

I got an internet charge on my Visa card
for a thousand bucks and I know it's too much
cause I ain't been to the web, I ain't been to the site
cause the avatars and pop-ups burn me all uptight.
Are you a boy? Are you a girl?
Are you a dog? Are you a squirrel?
Is a masquerade the method of the future net world?
Am I fly? Am I sly? Am I selling what you're buying?
Can you look me in the eye and tell me that I'm lying?

　　See my site at

　　　　revolution dot com
　　Send email

　　　　to una dot bomb

If the purpose of the worship of advanced technology
is to build a new community for you and you and me
then what is all the hustlin' tryin' to nail down a fraction
of a cut of the percentage in electric transaction?
Know it too that what you do, babe, and everything you be
is collected by the minions of the phone company.
In the silicon back alleyways no matter how you try
you can't leave -- you can't run -- you can't even die.
Nineteen eighty-four is really sixty four bits wide.

See my site at

      revolution dot com

Send email

      to una dot bomb

First, they have to listen in the name of fighting crime
Then it's secret backdoor courtrooms where you're guilty all
the time.
If you're having trouble sleeping, here's a thought to fill
your nights:
can you really buy security by giving up your rights?
Diamonds in red lasers, gold traces on green board
it's a microvolt landscape for the next world war.
Spiders sniff the internodes, hackers build dark life,
the battle's here already, but as silent as a knife.

See my site at

      revolution dot com

Send email

      to una dot bomb

OUTRO

O the moon is so round, but this is out too far and it gets too cold. The tall Douglas firs know it's noble to fast but hard to go hungry. In the summer there are ants in the kitchen, but the days didn't get carried away fast enough. To spite them I tried to build but there were still holes that didn't get fixed; then the tools became too heavy and I left them where they fell. Now the stove glows red with the last of the firewood, so I put on all my clothes, sit on the front step and try to make a plan.

One night a drunk teacher killed his wife in a car accident just a stone's throw away. I heard the crash and phoned in the emergency. I heard her call his name with her last breath but she was under the overturned Chevrolet and we could not reach her. Afterwards books lay scattered in the yard, the open pages fluttering like questions in the afternoon breeze.

One morning I realized that the road dead ended just ahead but I'd have to admit I'm lost before I could turn around, and you know me, stubborn as a bent nail.

The front door was almost my coffin lid, and for years afterwards I would drive by and see my ghost sitting on the front steps, head in hands, elbows on knees, as if only I could see a little further down into the dry and cobwebbed hole, there were a reason for all of it.

Louisa Calio

FINDING MYSELF AGAIN

This moment in time
is a mixing of ancient and modern styles
those who cling to the old Gods, vengeful and burning
stand beside those who know the God within
both are tempered by degrees of history.

Perhaps this journey is a recovery
lost parts of myself tied to an ancient past.
I came not to see him, but myself
the war is within
the part of me that dares to be free
that would not be trapped by material comforts
promises of success, all the rest.

Now is a greater wholeness, humility and peace
all things seem possible
Open, gentle
without the need to be beaten
or forced.

I still hear the voice within crying for love
it draws me to discover
recover all the lovers
I become pregnant with tomorrows.

Paula Camacho

CLASSMATE

she is dying
the news comes in an email
a gentle rain of words washing away hope
lungs liver bones hospice care

in the distance I hear her last breaths
see her round young face as it once was
the joy she spread to her classmates

I think of her my age
having to already let go of tomorrows

now it is time to prepare
allow the sun to show the way
while thoughts of her drift in and out
like passing prayers

LETTING GO

It is not by choice we let them go
those warm afternoons at little league games
those frigid days at a football field

my son did not know his great grandfather
how the taste of cream soda brings back
the smell of cherry pipe tobacco

my grandfather smoked until the age of eighty-five
the way he always had rock candy around
and change for the ice cream man

my son knew his own grandfather for only ten years
his special visits timed for baseball or football
lawn chair in hand, sideline encouragements ready

watch the ball, catch the ball
run, run, run, you can do it
afterwards a hardy *good job*

and in the wake of time where other beginnings start
eventually he had to let go of his grandfather's presence
and those warm afternoons at little league games

OBITUARY
    for Kathy

you leave quietly
the small obituary notice
full of family
beloved wife, mother, sister
cherished grandmother

missing from small print
your smiles, your sense of humor
the way you worked to make a life

now you join others in centuries gone
those who were part of the wisdom
not the famous, not the ones
whose names are forever known

but there you are
in the opening of spring
in the song of a robin
between the leaves of trees
when the moon is at its highest
in the laughter that lingers
in the world you left
missing you

STUDY OF WATER –LILIES 1908
Oil on canvas by Claude Monet

Green and yellow fill the eyes
water lilies arched by wild grass and shrubs
a walking bridge pinnacles the top half of the painting
beyond it, a growth of trees walling us in this one spot.

I blink as I stare at it
but focus remains somewhere in its past
forever in the eye of Monet
gone from him into brush and paint
canvas and carapace.

If I stood on that bridge
I would smell the warmth of a mild day
see the stream clearly choked with abundance
lush green filling the void everywhere
but the path to its existence is lost
this picture all that is left.

I see the weeping willow in the corner
and know why it is there.

TWO DAYS AFTER HER DEATH

I am here
The laundry is not a burden today
I ignore knee pain as I walk the stairs
Clean shirts on each arm
Down again three times to retrieve
Socks, pajamas, underwear
Sweaters, jackets
Replace summer clothes
Laid gently in boxes
I set the table
Think about each plate, fork and knife
As if for the first time
The minutes are taken up
Noticing each movement
I know I will not glory
In each breath as I do today
Tomorrow's routines will not be
As shiny
But for now I need
To feel each second
She cannot

Lynn Cooper

BORING SURPRISE

Inside a dumpy office
in the town of Anywhere I sit
a mature woman
in a grey dismal cubicle
wrapped in a cocoon of boredom
performing dull repetitive
detailed data entry
papers everywhere
wooden desk barely visible, like me

until a male employee
disrupts my monotony
takes notice of my
hair, hands, figure
feeds my ego
chocolate-dipped words
sends me honey-coated texts
lights an aging libido

Adriana DiGennaro

CITY LODGINGS

Plaster,
walls crack.

The kitchen sink with its two taps
trickling.

The lack of counterspace
and sticky dots of dried cran-grape.

The angry pile of cutlery, butterknife
and fork tine.

Dishwater smell, untouchable towel.
Mismatched drinking glasses.

Couch slumped,
cotton coming loose.

Outlets iced in white paint.
Little rugs never get cleaned.

Brass locks and neighbors,
Yes we have a corkscrew.

The heavy windows
and honking, walkers and mica glinting.

The resident rodent, rustling
when sounds fold up into silence.

GLITTER

riding the train   watching a couple   and her diamond

lump in my larynx   her diamond   her diamond

and their baby who's eating   small chunks of something

from a spill-proof cup   flexing feet in tiny ski boots
mushing its hand

onto its mother   my stormy face   I think of you   tall
and silent

with your red hair   and your Mexican girl   with a
harelip   and kid

that probably eats   small chunks of something   in the
house

you father them in   when you're not in New York   with
me   and my kicking

and clawing   at circumstance   never a ring   but
she has   none either

damn your daft inaction   her bare finger   my bare
finger

my bare heart   and do her eyes glitter   like mine   like
mine

JANUARY 28

From a west-facing window of the house
there are: snow-caked evergreens.

Tangled wood,
the homemade swing with its too-long ropes

looped around the broken oak branch.
And all things   faltering in a wind.

She is gone

but you're
a precious stone

you deserve a cottage among vineyards so north
that the steel waves of the Sound almost hit

Let's write you   a home
there it is, on the east end   of this poem

TANKA FOR A STRANGE SEASON

The sun fakes gold and excess heat as if
it's still summer, but she knows better, and
the trees know better: things really are dying.

She hides her head under the covers for
as long as possible before someone
gets angry at her. There's nothing she can do.

She dreams of a shaman healer. Of her
red eyes the healer interprets, you have
allergies. She says, I have blocked energies.

There's yellow and brown and red confetti
shimmering meanly in the yellow light,
rude and wishing everything away from it.

She goes to the outlet stores to shop in
October. She buys mom a gold compass
necklace and she gets herself a bag. Big deal.

These signs touting activities. It's just
people taking some pumpkins and apples
knowing full well the end is coming for them.

Every morning someone wakes up at five
and seven and nine and never really
sleeps. And she wakes up to coffee but boredom.

Sex happens but boredom returns and the
ground is still full of what's rotting. Those crows
still unzip the sky. The days get chopped in half.

And what a terrible thing to realize:
only the crows have laughed in these three months.
worse to wonder if she ever will again.

The torment starts in mid-august and doesn't let up
until the end of December when winter
has thoroughly replaced it.

Kathaleen Donnelly

IN THE CITY

I hear the rain
plopping into its own puddles
echoed in the dank tunnel
underneath Amsterdam and 9th.

Empty air
holds damp notes
as they slowly float
up and away.

The loneliness of that tunnel
follows me down
the drowning street
to my doorstep.

I look back
lost for words of relief
having left those sounds and smells
behind me.

LOST IN AUTUMN

Dry leaves
crackle underfoot
in a forest of
fallen songs.

Gray clouds
hover overhead
in a sky of
remembered dreams.

Morning rain
brightens tired browns
in a puddle of
spoken words.

Misty drizzle
lingers midair
in a sea of
thoughts undone.

THE DIG

Blydenburg Park
this hot midsummer's day
calls me to its waters' edge,
soft light breeze tall pines shade
moss-covered stones.

I wander worn dirt paths,
drawn towards rush of river,
its belly full of living beings
breathing.

Earth disturbed
by centuries of seasons,
tear in its skin, I dig deeper,
a satchel, a find, a link to the past.

Arrowheads no owner to claim,
I examine my inheritance.

Did a young brave hide it here,
drop it unaware, lose it,
unable to retrace his steps,
frustrated, gave up the search,

the way I do my keys?

Walter Donway

SPEAK THEIR NAMES, ONCE MORE
(Las Vegas shooting Oct. 1, 2017)

Recite, now, 59 names—is it more?
And then. 500 names, just give or take.
For you and I, today, have kept that score
Of dead, dying, wounded. But for their sake.

Make for me, one more time, the sounds of names
A mother at dusk called to them at play,
Who bleed, now, from their individual veins,
Have died, or die, or cry in pain, this day.

Repeat their names that I may listen
To sounds a lover murmured as sleep came on;
I cannot bear the entombed silence, when
The shots, sirens, pleas, curses, screams are gone.

Pretty legs in cowboy boots to turn a head,
An autumn evening sweet, a country song:
Each small happiness assassinated—
A world in which it does not now belong.

So, will you say their names that I may hear
Echoes of some friend phoning, who might say,
In words that then we did not hold so dear,
"Just needed to hear your voice, today."

THE AGE OF YEATS

I look to a November cold this year
Not with the season, but with memory;
For William Yeats, a poet whom I love,
Died at the age I'll reach—seventy-three.

A boy, I clambered over stones with him,
At dusk, to flick a fly onto a stream
To lure a shadow trout and there below
Saw horns, dim horns, the moon pale as a dream.

With Yeats, I heard leaves flutter love in May,
As one dear woman led me by a lake;
But October's frost bowed us down with sounds
Reproachful, fleeing steps in dry leaves make.

We heard ideals so long in their creation
Slurred by the lips of low, most sordid men,
Learned that death demands a generation
To bleed, let blood, for them to live, again.

And how each age may crave to close that rent
Between the heavens and the straw-strewn bed,
That Crazy Jane and Wild Old Men want all
Body gives to body when pride is shed.

How learned men ascend a winding stair
To see fine things they thought, when young,
But borrowed toys, have risen in their gyres
So nightfall now with lanterns bright is strung.

Peter V. Dugan

SUSPENDED SENTENCE

Is this where you held court?

Out in the woods,
in the clearing
surrounded by nature,
the judge's chamber
and jury box, above,
in the trees.

You were sentenced
to life without parole,
    no mercy,
        no appeal,
            no lo contenderé.

Condemned to dangle
            between
        heaven and earth,
by the string of lies
            tangled
with knots of truth.

Was there any reasonable doubt?

Beneath the bough
of the tree
the rope lays strewn
on the ground,
uncoiled like the carcass
of the serpent cast
out of the garden.

Are you free now?

DAEDELUS' STEP-DAUGHTER

Angela climbed to the roof
of the apartments and spread
her wings to fly away.

She longed to be a butterfly
gliding across a wildflower
meadow, free on the breeze
of a sunny day.

But, she fluttered
like a moth,
back and forth,
boys, alcohol,
and drugs.

So, she leapt for the sky
but, the bushes
broke her fall.

"Why?"
"Because it was raining
and I wanted to see the sun."

Nursed back to health,
in a fog of 'happy pills,'
she said she saw the light.

She finished the vial;
and smiled,
"I don't need these anymore."
and found a taller
building.

ANOTHER BROTHER, GONE

Another hole in my heart.

Together we shared a bike,
our youth, our coming of age,
a friendship through our teens
and adulthood.

We worked together, played together
and partied together.
We shared a love of music, art, black
leather jackets, cars and bikes.
We rocked and rolled
with the Grateful Dead and the Rolling Stones.

From hanging out at the shopping center
or the Inn, to Something Blue and Cousins.
From adventures in Long Beach
to misadventures in New Paltz;

we shared a brotherhood.

Time and distance have no meaning.
Now you're just a little farther away.
We can pick up where we left off.
I'll meet you on that Highway
in the Great Beyond
and we'll have a good time
when I get there.

I miss you, Jerry.
Ride In Peace.

STILL WAITING

It's another family Thanksgiving.

Dinner's finished, Mom's in the kitchen
with the girls cleaning up, and the kids
are running around the house playing,

Dad and the rest of the guys are watching
football and I am expecting you to walk
through the door with some lame excuse
as to why you weren't here on time.

But I don't care about that.
I just want to talk to you.
I want to tell you about Lisa and Kevin.
I want to talk about my book and new poems.
I want to share golf stories, the good shots,
bad shots and the would've, could've, should've
great scores we never get or ever had.

I want to know what you've been doing.
I want to hear about your work and the bar scene.
I want you to tell me about your new girlfriend
or the old one you're still seeing.
I want to hear about your poems and the story
you still haven't finished yet.

I look over at your picture on the fireplace mantle.
You look good dressed in a tuxedo for a wedding,
a dance or whatever it was, I forget.
But, your picture hides the 4x12 inch black
box that hold your ashes.

Alex Edwards-Bourdrez

RESTORATION

I've replaced the rhyme in verse
With tattered lines of random sound.
I've replaced my faith in God
—Never very galvanized nor well regarded
By those I hold in high regard—
With troves of desperate hope.

I've replaced my quickened vision
—However fleeting, blinding, exciting,
Or soberly considered it may have been—
With worn-out tapestries of memories
And pools of washed-out watercolors.

Then, at times as now, I see:
Writing verse is like a seizure—
Freezing time enough for me
To shape a moment at my leisure.

THE SAME TECHNICIAN

His cut above the ears
Betrayed a bit of gray.
A wizened thicker skin
Now hung around those eyes
As kind as I recalled.

His gait still soft and sure,
He noiselessly approached
The waiting vein I'd placed
Exposed for him to probe
As gently as before.

Just as he said, "You'll feel
A pinch," he gave a smile.
I glanced expectantly.
The burn lived short as I,
Who'd slipped his memory.

Sasha Ettinger

BENDING LIFE WITH WORDS

My nature was sluggish
    like something eating its way through a leaf.
I moved through life by instinct.
      When no path suited me,
           I found my own.

I bend life with words,
    expand and collapse time.
I reshape a childhood that never unfolded neatly,
    locate a sister who left no heart prints behind,
rewrite a mother
    whose life was lost when forgetting
      bleached it away.

My poems slide like an otter down a slope
    from one stanza to another.
  I walk into a hothouse of impossibility,
      fill crevices,
        smooth scars,
          then move on.

FOUND MEMORIES

Beyond the window,
    lured by the moon's cool light,
        I re-invent the rooms of my childhood.

I walk for miles on steady roads,
        wrap thoughts around swaggering hills,
    trail butterflies through brigades of wildflowers,
        delight in maples' wagging crimson tongues.

      With cupped hands,
I chase fireflies in wooded thickets,
        my golden braids swinging pendulums
          across the slim of my back.

When summer sun hangs low,
      I swim in nearby streams,
    minnows the size of silver dimes
      between my toes.

      My youth trusting the last of sunlight
      as it moves away.

Joseph Greco

UNTITLED

When she was pregnant with Watt, Rachel needed work.
All she could do then was candle eggs.
She sat for hours in the dark,
bent over a conveyor belt transporting row after row of eggs
lit from beneath so they glowed in the darkness like clock faces
or the heads of saints.
Doing this day after day she cultivated a loneliness
that defied anyone to look more deeply.
Just then she thought of her own mother.[1]
"Santa's a pedophile," she told her once.
"What's a pedophile?" Rachel asked.
"Just never you mind," she said. "Do your sums," she said.
All told, Momma was what you'd call a fatalist.[2]
Do you mean to tell me you thought it all through
and concluded there is no God?
She must look now for a blood spot in the yellow.
She looked and looked until that was all she saw.
Even in her dreams,
she never saw the egg,
only the speck of red in the bright yellow.
The red told her the egg was no good—
not fit for human consumption.
Those eggs she marked with a black dot.
She did not know what became of them,

---

[1] In her story, as in her conversation, Rachel's mind wanders freely. This habit of mind is called 'intertexuality.'—Editor's Note

[2] Any struggle to connect with the past is a lost cause.—R. Caul

whether any non-human ever ate them.
Momma and I never did see eye to eye.
She expected me to be like her.
Of course I wasn't.
That was either a blessing or a curse.
At the end of the day
Rachel walked into the green twilight

where figures hung etched in ink.
She'd leave that place slightly more
disconnected from life.
Where was I going?
She saw on others' faces happiness and ambition,
emotions she could not remember ever feeling.
I cannot reconcile the fact that I am the one
who experienced this event I am now remembering.
Her feet were swollen, but she'd walk[3] home
swinging her purse like Julie Christie.
Even while pregnant
she was tall and commanding.
"She moves slowly," they would say.
But that has less to do with fatigue
than with the knowledge that people will wait for her.
She didn't need Freud to realize
the urge to transcend the past
might itself be determined by the past.
To herself she'd think: If I were free, if I were free.
And then remember, no, she wasn't alone.
Her life was in ruins, yes,
a consequence of biology.
She had no plan to rescue it.

---

[3] shanks' mare

A voice said, "But it's April, Rachel"
No, No, I mustn't.
The tragedy of her life was that she walked on pavement
when the only thing she loved was grass.
If I've done wrong, I'm dying for it now.
Watt left me, but I don't blame him.
I forgive him.
Forgive *me?*
Banish him from your thoughts, love.
He's nothing but a bird of bad omen.

Leonard Greco

EULOGY II
For Joey (Stymie) D'Angelo

I remember his words
told to me
so many years ago

words now
dust covered and ashen

that no man could
scrawl his eulogy
not on stone
nor from a pulpit

and I recall thinking
we are so young
with so much ahead
why worry about
such things

and he laughed
so much like Scratch
and said

this life offers no
solace in aging
in withering
and dying

dry like rotted prunes
give me the fast lane
he said

and
the fast lane
claimed
his soul —

FADED GLORY

Breakfast with old friends from
days gone by, remembering
who we were, dismissing
who we might have become

It is a flash of past glory
that each of us rides,
reaching perhaps for infinity

Hey, we were something then

Hard guys to be
reckoned with

Warriors fearlessly facing
all comers

A cold winter's morning,
breaking bread with old friends,
staring eyes glazed,
touched gently by realization

We may no longer be
masters of
our former glory

BOBBY TOOTH REVISITED
per cugino mio

they tell me you are
no longer who
you once were and
are not likely to
ever be

these are words I
wish not to hear

you
once my mentor
       protector
       brother
on those hardscrabble
streets we roamed

kings were we

our throne
a swaggering
sidewalk gait

kings no longer

that throne now
empty

as empty as
alcohol drenched memories —

HAVE I BLAMED MY FRIENDS?

Tommy still knows how to laugh. He jokes
about kids and the trash they talk
the way the ballers did when we were young
and thought we still could play and still
accepted we were goons. But Sam no longer sees
the world that way, posting pictures of his kids
in suits and gowns, with awards and pins
for feats beyond their years. Sam is gray.
Hell, aren't we all? But you forgive it
when one of us distracts you with
a risqué story of being twenty-five.

How do I feel about having to say
I wish my friends who are still alive
could live to distract us all? Not to say
I want them to live in the past. Just to say
I think we can feel ourselves alive.
We can talk our trash to kids
coming up, because of who they are:
the thinner us with less experience.

But who am I to say it's no less dignified
to act the fool at fifty-five than dance
like buffoons at the back of a dive
where we looked each other in the eyes
as the music drowned all thought
but we are young and good times never die.

MY PERSONAL HISTORY OF YOU

You're the Annie Phillips of your generation.
that girl around the corner, the Mr. Googles
of my lost toys. When you leave you are
the high school centerfielder
who ran down my long fly ball,
but you also help my mother
as she sledges a kitchen wall to dust
while my father patrols the streets.

You're standing by my side as we wash and dry
the stemware at the Sunday Tavern, lending me
money for months I borrow rent.
As I lie in darkness you sing me through fear
to a distant infinity more frightening than death.
You are the day I stopped going to church.
If you sharpen the spikes of the abbey fence
I thrust my hands upon, I'll never tell.

That year instead you hand me the leash
I use to lead my best friend down a city block
fifteen years long. You polish those bared teeth,
then lower the dark lips over them for good.
Once he's gone you wed me to a Midwest girl
at the borough hall, a daughter of German twine,
the Wilma Dineen of an inland shore, who floats
our tiny ship on a glycerin sea.

You sign divorce papers while I picket, and broker
the adoption that costs me a fortune to learn
sacrifice for someone else's fate.
You are my self-assessment in triplicate,
my hiring and firing, my retirement. You are
Florida, a beach I roam, my metal detector
as I scour dunes for broken runes of you.

Aimee Herman

CONSEQUENCE OF QUIETUDE

imagine a slice of paper.
the edges have yet to reach an erection—
laying flat.

she is this:
wooden, worn down to splinter-type.
turquoise veins to salivate consciousness.

her size is not quite exact.
she is torn down the middle to allow
                    access of.

man-made ink enclosure pushes.
misspells several verbs and notes.
does not wait for documented answer.

imagine the hidden curves behind spackle, or.
tubes of organic scriptures.
bleeding within her.

somewhere against the spine.
and beneath speech terminal.
her no has disappeared.

LOST MEMBRANE

if only you could trace your steps back to where you were
when you had it last, it might find its way back to you—
she said.

were you riding your bike,
with stool shaped like a tear drop drinking your seated skin?
fingers curled, praying to palms of tightness?

and did the circular motion of distance
cause you to forget the evolution of grain against
pavement?

maybe the metal beneath you enraged your pores,
your clefts   your fissured femalia.

do you miss it?

what about signs, reports—
interviews of those last to see it?

a paper trail?
blood trail?

could it have been a break-in?
recall setting or temperature.

                    *

the ground spoke autumn, though
I believed in snow back then.

I believed in undisclosed shapes and
experimental angles.
that ice can be a meal or artistic drip against
window panes.
his skin was made of eyelashes and
windchimes.
delicate drapery of stitched blinks, swaying.

silent.   Except for a knee-bend or lip rub.
his torso read backwards and basin of bones
bred nourishment.

he asked.
but said it'd never return.

sometimes things are meant to disappear   in order
to understand the meaning of their existence.

Joan Higuchi

COMMUNION DRESS

She stitched it patiently
each piece of lace
with every other
interfaced to form

a parasol of skirt that
sent me twirling—
delighted in the way
that it went swirling

like a dancer's tutu
made of sea foam
or some other
insubstantial froth.

I hardly could contain
my glee that special day.
I vowed to keep that
precious gift forever

you gave it away.

NO CHANCE NOW

Clasped within my arms, you slowly
slid away. I willed your feeble breath
to draw once more, like bow
across your instrument of voice
without effect.

Whispering my love
I watched your skin tone fade
to shades of gray, while eyes
the tint of winter-colored skies
fixed on the window blackened
by night, traced there a scene
that only you could see

waiting...

until she came and you felt
free to leave. That window
held a different view for me

the place where flowers grew
in weed-thinned rows
that you checked every morning
for emerging bloom

the wall where Anne and I
played after school

thumping our ball and waking you
from sleep you needed
for your night-time work.

I never thanked you for your gift
of flowers... of many things
and wish somehow our thumping ball
could once more rouse you now.

Vicki Iorio

I LOST MY CELL PHONE

My little red candy box is gone.
Where did you go?
How did you get there?
How did you escape from me?

You were way better than a husband
vibrating in my pocket
safeguarding my secrets
red lighting my calls straight to voice mail.

Are you rolled up in the sheets of another?
Another I could speed dial IF I had a phone!

Were you flushed away at an altitude of 30,000 feet?
Are you free falling back to earth in a pee ice cube?

Should I call the police and hint at murder?
They can track you down tower to tower.
I know how they do it
I watch True Crime on Spinster TV.

If I cry out for my cherry love will you be turned on?
Do I even want you anymore?

I'm drinking again.
Verizon cannot console me with their minimal fees
and corrections.

Like a man you've disconnected.
Marriage and cell phones both come down to the fine print.

Next time I'll try a Blackberry.
Forbidden fruit.

AFTER YOUR APARTMENT CAUGHT FIRE ON ARLINGTON ST.

those closest to you teased that I started the fire
with my mind, a type of untraceable arsonist
armed with only the intensity of my resentment for you.

we stood in the charred hallway and stared
at all your burnt belongings, your collected years
of junk, crisped and soggy from flame then hose.

I traced our initials on the blackened walls;
a ritualistic offering you did not comprehend
and when you started to cry, I searched for the champagne
we were going to open when things got better.

you watched as it dribbled down my chin and knew
somewhere within your soft bones the truth in their
teases,
of my knowledge of her, of your deserved incineration.

something they don't warn others about betraying
daughters who didn't know motherly love:

> we do not hesitate to strike the match
> for we taught ourselves to fire walk
> and are accustomed to the taste of ash.

WHAT IS KEPT

this is how my red hair glowed on your chest
this is the reason we picked corner tables
this is after I burned the vodka sauce
this is when I collected pebbles for the dead
this is your diamond-shaped freckle I love
this is how I matched your mother's scream
this is how I stood naked in your arms
this is why I never could enter to the left
this is how we made love on the beach
this is the sound you would always make
this is the color you painted over the dents
this is how I stopped before she began
this is the moment I laid down in the street
this is how I dissolved our child into mush
this is our life in a small basement studio
this is why I never used cinnamon
this is how we slept better intertwined
this is how you are the one I measure against
this is being each a lesson learned
this is what remains after years
this is the reason love is a sculptor
this is how trinkets are made

TO A LOVER RETURNING AFTER 12 YEARS

we do not know what it will be like
but I have a premonition of annihilation:
a leveling cloud spreading out slow
deliberate and deadly, blocking out sun and moon.
the same, I imagine, as how you'll touch me
taking back what has never not been yours
and how, when you finally reach the reactor,
that red ripened cunt in final countdown,
there will be sudden heat and blinding light
followed by pulsed silence
followed by both of our ends.

Peter Thabit Jones

INTERNAL ELEGIES

This is the low tide
Of the mind,
The debris
Stuck in a dead bay's mud.

This is the litter of thoughts
Broken on a hard day's rocks,
Wreckage of the heart
That the birds don't want.

The calming sea
Is so far out,
And the narrative says
It won't come back.

This is the life's
Tall heavy sky,
Torn pillows of clouds
Dumped on the horizon's
Fall-edge of words.

Internal elegies
Have gathered
(Grey, graveyard, grey),
A living father
A lost son.

LESSON

The jackdaws, time's watchers,
Squat on the roofs
Above the traffic.

Their night eyes
Send their reports in sepia.
I sit in my car

Stopped by new road-works.
Then it's down the motorway,
The March morning sun

Blasting the steelworks
Like some kind of warning.
I teach my lesson,

Waiting for you to come.
The afternoon over,
I drive towards home,

My thoughts of you
Not coming unfolding
Through the miles.

Something is broken,
Has been taken away.
A closeness,

Once like new clothes,
Has been dragged up to the sky,
With the dark rags of jackdaws

Littering the evening.

MOTHER

From your weakness
Came my strength.

From your black and white
Came my colours.

From your denial of me
Came my belief in me.

From all your lies
Came my search for truths.

From your cold looks
Came the fire in my eyes.

From your lack of hugs
Came my tenderness.

From your lack of touch
Came my need to feel life.

From your lack of kisses
Came my lips wanting dreams.

From your street of false games
Came my cities of hope.

From your selfish road
Came all of my paths.

From your milk untasted
Came my thirst for love.

From your unspoken words
Came my poet's voice.

POETRY READING, THE ROBERT FROST FARM

September grieves in me;
My child, lost, shines
In the New Hampshire afternoon.

Words leave my mouth,
Weighted as apples
On a tree; words farmed

Long ago in a room
In Swansea, damp
With a coffined silence.

I read to people
I will *never reach*.
We are all in shadows.

A poem is not a step
In one's ambition;
The drama of it

Is not an act
To get *somewhere*.
'I am a singer merely,

I sing my song'.
Something there is
In me

That loves a wall,
The separation
From others.

'No more heroes,
No more dreams,
Life's what it is,

Not what it seems'
I wrote long ago
When the stars fell down.

And how their child lost,
Robert's and Eleanor's,
Shines in my mind.

Their folding
Of the clothes
No longer needed;

The falling emptiness;
The 'why?' crying
Through the heart's universe,

The scream of the blood
That the staring eyes shed.
Grief, a visitor,

In the rooms of the head.
Something there is
In me

That loves a wall,
The separation.
My words,

Their words, fall
Like apples
When there

Is no-one around,
And the air, natural as God,
Consumes the song.

FIRST HOUSE

you alone in your first house
you alone find the bones of a squirrel
its furry tail intact
patient and alone in the empty attic of your first house
and you alone make intermittent love with borrowed men
and you alone hear the nickering of ghost horses in the barn
and the cold sky hovers like a banker's suit
over your first house
and you alone understand what the barstool historians
meant
when they spoke about your first house
and why it may be your last house too.
You alone are cognizant that it's 19 miles to Patchogue
and 78 miles to Springs from your first house
a half-mile from the train station
a decade away from tragedy
a distant remove of tears
and you are triangulating the distances between all that
and this first house
where small maple trees grow in gutters
and mold is eating the plaster
and insects are eating the floorboards
and you alone paint walls and closets
shimmering flower colors in your first house,
and it's yours, all yours, your choice, your taste, your
headache.
and your car radio plays the ambitious violin craziness of
Bach's second partita
giving you agita as you pull away from your first house

down the red pebble driveway you love more than a person
leaving your house but only to do a few things that need
doing
and then to return.
And you alone are evolving into who knows what
and you alone are nesting
finally in a place you found and chose all by yourself
and the house sparrows pause on the portico and flick their
heads and wings
side to side
little and grey
chirp chirping and heedlessly alive and pleased to be so
and the mourning doves dodge and flush each other out of
the privets
and coo in that call they make which sounds sad to our ears
but probably not to theirs
and the spring smell of dirt fills your lungs with its promise
and the sinews of grapevines look like your strong muscular
grapevines
and they are
all yours
yours alone

LOST AND FOUND

Weekends, I approach my yard with tools
and a mission, meaning to find:
Amelia Earhart. Meaning. Peace of mind.
Bits of my lost selves:
The ponytailed five-year-old
whose black Scottie
(my first love, silky black with his
best-dressed red-and-green plaid belly)
slid down between the bed and the wall
of an Ontario bed and breakfast.
The quote-ruby-unquote birthstone ring that
squirmed out of a beach bag at Cedar Beach.
The sunhat from Korvette's that an August breeze
scooped out from the trunk
of our white Plymouth Valiant—
it had a push-button transmission—
at the old Orient Inn. (It had been
quite the glamorous hat. Once, the inn
had been glamorous too.)
Flotsam from
the South Shore's last safe childhood,
places and things that we leave
or that leave us. Like the last Christmas present
from my mother, the bracelet I slept in
till waking one morning to an empty wrist.

It must be here somewhere,
the last token of someone's love,
maybe my last token of love, period.
A memory and a fear, all here.
I rake the driveway, sifting in gravel,
panning for gold.

THE GEOGRAPHY OF LOSS

is an old and still and very big thing,
a geography of flatness and lacks
like for one a lack of elevation
its markers show no real movement
enabling one to map it
here a glacial moraine of
small emotional pitfalls
there abruptly a lake without bottom or beach
no waves of grief to erode its shoreline
no dizzying peaks of hysteria
no treelines outside the city of ghosts
a metropolitan area of the missing
beyond plains of dimly remembered
pain under the longitude-latitude grid
denoting degrees of emptiness the only movement
underground streams of sorrow
coursing beneath the stasis of pine barrens
ringed by phragmites
those cockroaches of the marsh
doing what they do best:
filling in the empty patches
and the grey ribbon roadways
tie place-name to place-name
with more verve than the bereaved
the volcano is spent
there will be no lava

Carolyn Mary Kleefeld

FAITH

The wisteria vine is winter clad,
every bud containing a mystery
tightly in its fold.
What will happen in the spring
it cannot know.

Like a transparent mist,
Faith lingers as a possibility
for those who hesitate,
quivering in the unknown.

Ignited by the precious memory
of last year's glorious bloom,
Faith can come forth
at any moment,
transfusing the lost
lighting their path forward.

HAIL SPRING

Today's world is a surreal circus
with its crude behaviors
so blatantly exposed,
particularly now in the mad arena
called politics.

We have reached the eleventh hour
in this cycle of deterioration,
with the contagion of violence spreading.

There are too many robots
numbly steering,
too many Barbie dolls
setting the pace on CNN,
making horrific announcements
with dead faces.

The human touch
has been lost to the chaos,
and the "substantial," deftly ignored.

Hail spring;
it's time for re-invention.

TRAVELING NEW WORLDS
for DC

Disoriented and lost,
I climb into
your golden arms—
my world re-found.

There, in the warmth
of your arms,
a glory is replenished.

Enraptured in the spell
of our wedded hearts,
we wander in the Mystery.

You are always
within me now,
my sky-eyed angel—
with wings of iridescence.

Borne by passion's flight,
we travel new worlds,
side by side
weaving ourselves into history.

Denise Kolanovic

A MOMENT OF CLARITY

I cannot lose what is rightfully mine!
I said it to the universe.
No reply. But, lately, the law
of divine compensation
is forthwith.

THE SMELL OF SUN TAN LOTION

I was in the pharmacy
And I heard "The Sweetest Hangover"
By Diana Ross as I searched the aisles
For sun tan lotion.
There was such an array
That I had to open them up
So I could remember that scent:
The one that made me remember
Manhattan Beach in 1974.
I can almost feel the sand on my feet
And hear the laughter of my teenage
Friends as we toss the beach ball around.
If only I could be back there for a moment.

ZUMBA

The salsa beat
pulses through me like a bolt
of lightening!
Though I can't translate
all the words,
It does not matter.
I feel my Latin ancestors' songs:
swirl and dash,
step together and jump:
duhduhduhduh duh da
dudduhduh duh da.
I slap my rump three times
And turn to the other side.
Repeat, repeat!

Beverly E. Kotch

PURPLE HEART

On Christmas day, my true love
Gave to me
A purple heart, a damaged heart
Badly scarred
An eerie reflection of his own

On this day, I note the flaws
Bent setting of silver
Crushed stone etched with pain
See blocked lobes straining 'gainst the wall

Yes, this year
This symbol of his mended, broken heart
Is by far the best gift
I could have gotten

MEMORY DISTILLED

Rising tide of venom
Open mouth
Drown in
River of hate

Rub salt in
Open wound
Spill childhood
Secrets

Blunt silence

Odor of memory
Festers

Sound of doors
Slamming

Open bottles
Shots of sarcasm
Tumblers full of
Natural slaughter

Death
Slumped over
Behind the
Wheel

CHILDHOOD LOST

Every moment
Movement
Monitored

Every childish
Desire game idea
Carefully controlled

Every dream
Detoured
Devoured

Every chance
At individuality
Stolen

Norbert Krapf

FIGHTING WITH ANGELS

Fighting with angels
is a losing proposition.

Their bones do not break.
Their egos rarely balloon.
They never rise to an insult
because their position
in the pantheon is assured.
They never grow weary
because the engine beneath
their long flight is full
of eternal approval.

You want to punch them out
and your fist goes through cloud.
Most infuriating of all, what's
on their side is almost always God.
Their knowing smile gives it away.

Me, I've had enough of this.
Angels don't speak my language.
Don't tell me about the one
you say must be my guardian.
She gave up on me long ago,
though she pretends to care.
She has other ladders to climb.

I like keeping my altitude low.
I'm learning to live on the street.
Gutter talk is my new mother tongue.

127

HOLDING ON AND LETTING GO

Little one, I'm holding on to you
as I'm letting go of someone else,
a great-uncle you'll never meet.

As he slips away, barely able
to breathe and unable to
give voice to his words

your voice is coming into
your mouth to give shape
to what you will say to the world.

Across a dark ocean from you
I'm listening for your emerging voice
to sing me into the morning

as the brother of your grandmother
fades listening to the coming night.
I listen to both of you in your worlds

coming and going in different directions
as I sit up in bed absorbing the hushed
silence of this pre-dawn Thanksgiving Day

and give thanks for both your lives
as I move in his direction but savor
the light rising in your opening eyes.

INDIANAPOLIS ELEGY

Speak to me from the realm of angels
in vernacular but come down to me
on these streets. Talk to me of loss

of innocence back in the days when
priests ruled the Roman Catholic world
and you witnessed the fall from above.

Come down to my level, angel love.
Walk with me on these messy streets.
How could you so easily absent yourself

from my sacred protection? Did you not
feel the slightest compunction to intervene
when the Man of God had his way with boys

not yet risen to the power of the almighty No?
How did it feel to let go of your guardianship?
Was that you I heard whimpering from above?

Where were you when I needed your care?
When prayer aborted in my youthful mouth?
When I started to sing what I now call the blues?

Why don't you come on down to me now?
It's not too late for this boy to receive angel love.
We'll learn how to sing together in tongues.

INVISIBLE GIFT TO AND FROM A SISTER

Sister, I send you
a gift for those never
allowed to breathe
in this world.

I send you one
breath of human love
from a brother left
behind in this world.

Never could I stop
sending you this gift
of my breath I wish
you could feel here.

Marilyn is your name.
Mary Lou is your sister.
Norbert, Edgar, and Leonard
are your brothers.

I would have us here
breathe together toward
you in a spiritual morse
code of those still living

in our world to say
that your breath from
yours comes to us
in ours as blind love.

LITTLE GIRL LOST BLUES

Brother wants to sing you something low down and blue.
Sis, he wants to sing you something low down and blue.
You got to know it all comes back to losing you.

Should he sing you Baby Please Don't Go?
Do you want to hear Baby Please Don't Go?
Answer's got to be Why No, Brother, No!

Brother, tell me I ain't been gone now sixty years.
Brother, how could it be I been gone sixty years?
Since I was born and died same time, not sixty years!

The good news, Sis, is that what's lost can be found.
The good news, Sis, is you were lost but now are found.
Now that brother found you he can see you all around.

Sister's in the sky and the land and the sea.
Sister's in the sky and the land and the sea.
Sister's spirit lives right here inside me.

Neil Leadbeater

LEAVING NEW STREET

Beyond the tunnels there were factories and cranes, a compendium
of car parks, junk yards, tips; bulldozers shifting history.
Tower blocks bestrode the landscape. The Monday wash,
draped over railings, dried in the midday heat.

Along the way, a series of signs in quick succession
told us where we were at: *Smethwick Rolfe Street –
Smethwick
Rolfe Street – Smethwick Rolfe Street –*
The summer haze, airless and venal, congealed with the log-
jam of
trade:
foundries, lighting and switchgear; dossils, plugs and valves;
they put back in place all those things
that I thought I had nearly lost: the smell of malt from a
Midlands brewery,
the red marl of the back-to-backs; a school bell in a
comprehensive
ringing me back to Maths.

I lived here once, much as I lived in other towns
but none has brought me back so much as this –
nosing the scent of something gone,
the past we always miss.

Maria Lisella

DEAD ROSE

Disbelieving he would never move,
I rubbed his shirtfront, startled
at the wood hardness beneath
pressed cotton, a mannequin of a dad.
Before he left the room,
I removed the glasses
tried to slip them into his jacket pocket,
where they sat most of the time.
Heard something crush,
my fingers were covered
with dry, papery, brown flecks
I recovered the dead white rose
I pinned to his lapel eight months ago
when we danced at my cousin's wedding.

WILD ONE

I press the accelerator pedal
ride close enough to read
Harley boy's helmet
Yuck Fou.
Skinny ankles, white sox
silver ponytail whips.
In mid-20s I might have
driven off the road
for him. Now,
as old as he,
we have too much
in common.

Maria Manobianco

BEST SAID PLANS

We planned for tomorrow,
not knowing what the day would bring
Hope was our armor, guiding the way
Time holds the upper hand on what must come to be

The sun filled the hospital room,
I sat at the foot of his bed
We spoke of healing time, being ready to go home
We planned for tomorrow,
not knowing what the day would bring

Soon he became restless,
discomfort dimmed his smile
I notified the Head Nurse
who reassured me, he was fine
Hope was our armor, guiding the way

He said, *I'm too tired for visits of any kind*
I listened and didn't visit
not knowing it was the end
Time holds the upper hand on what must come to be

LOST CONNECTION

I walk in the shadow
of tall buildings
in the city where I was born
I search for familiar faces
relatives, friends, neighbors
I find blank expressions
blind to my presence

I go to places once shared
Tony's Ice Cream Parlor
Mario's Pizza
The Boys and Girls Club
on 29th Street
find new buildings
in their place

I kneel in the church
where I was confirmed
and married
families and friends
filling every pew

I search for vibrations
that say, *welcome*
feel nothing
only shadows

ROCK OF AGES

As a child, I found it difficult to ignore
a stone or rock of unusual shape or color
like a heart, a round, or oval
I selected the smaller stones for my aquarium

As a teenager traveling to different places
I collected larger stones noted
where they were from and placed them
in the flower beds in my backyard

As I matured into womanhood, I appreciated
the significance of their ageless presence
They surrounded us and supported the ground
beneath our feet, and the magnificent buildings
and monuments that seem to touch the sky
The very core of our planet earth's integrity
is sustained by molten rock

Ancient cultures considered rocks sacred
eternal, and sacrificial. The scriptures referred
to David placing a small stone in a sling-shot
and conquering the giant, Goliath
saving the nation of Israel from the Philistines

As a senior, I place a small stone
on my husband's granite gravestone

Maria Matthiessen

BLOOD TEARS

I hid behind a rusty barrel
playing hide and seek
with brothers
and sister
on Mtwara beach.

The oldest, Peter,
came towards me -
I shrieked and ran,
tearing my ankle
on a rusty shard.

Blood gushed.
I was raced home
to my father who
put three staples in
my Achilles heel.

It hurt, yet I
was proud
that my father
could repair me.

DISGUISES

When I was six more than anything
I wanted to be a boy.
It was easy in Africa because I wore
my brother's shorts, a khaki shirt,
white socks and brown lace ups.

The boys seemed so free,
shot guns, mud brick walls,
allowed to go off on their own
leaving us out and anyway
my sister was a bit of a whiner.

I must have persuaded my mother
to cut my hair, because there it is
in photographs, straight, short,
parted neatly on the side.

I was startled once
at the club when I approached
The Ladies and a man said:
In here sonny boy, I ran away
red in the face.

I cut off my hair again at thirteen
and slicked it back
when my mother died untowardly.
It seemed easier to be a boy again.
No sissy tears, boys are allowed
to be silent; they don't like to be hugged.

JB McGeever

DAUGHTER

Young black girl of Brooklyn
The realtor says our neighborhood
Is fashionable

But there's a bottle of urine
Outside your bedroom window

Troubled men babble on the sidewalk
And that old man was shot in the head
Just a block away from your pillow

This one robbed the grocery store
That one stabbed outside the Tot Lot
Where you're learning to share

Young black girl of Brooklyn
I have a student who looks just like you
A biracial girl in this County of Kings

the boys call her that light-skinned bitch

At her desk she sucks her thumb
Then pulls a piece of cloth from her satchel
To rub it back and forth while she breathes

140

Daughter, I fear we met too late
All I can offer is a Lion in the Fall

But my mane will stay thick
My fangs and claws as sharp as any man's knife

Queen of Kings, I promise
These pretenders to the throne will not harm you

D. H. Melhem

POLAR ICECAPS

I'm holding on to the rail, the ride is so fast.

—Colette Inez

Yes—let's hold on tightly as we watch
the waters rise from melting polar icecaps
where bears float off on floes abducting them—
mystified, diving toward caverns of the sea.

And at an aftertime we'll wonder, too
(a trifle late) where we should emigrate
and just how far inland, and whether erratic
weather there will lose a feral vengeance
like downtown floods we fled to higher ground
uptown, and now once more must flee, abandoning
submerged real estate and soggy towers,
address of sharks and whales and bloated bears
and plankton's avid genes where we began
and might begin again, and then might not.

SEWING BASKET

I open my sewing basket and the word pops out
like a skein of air:
Mommy.
I'm five? thirty? fifty?
Ageless yearning
follows you down a footpath
winding the distance
between us.
It threads round your seamless image
I still inhabit.
That double inflection,
its pull and power, affection
stronger than time, strong as life.

Edmund Miller

POEM FOUND ELSEWHERE

A long-lasting, crisp,
exhilarating scent that
gives a man the
physical advantage.
Well-placed, it can be
your most effective
weapon.

POEM FOUND IN BED WHERE THEY LAY

TO OPEN
• SLIT OPEN ON THREE SIDES
• PULL BACK WRAPPER AND REMOVE SLICES
• REPLACE WRAPPER FOR PROTECTION

SNAPSHOT

Your picture's just fallen to the floor
denting its fake gold frame,
and now the glass is broken,
and I can see you only there
behind the cracks again. Really
I'd forgotten all about it. But
it seems it had been resting
on my desk since you left
whenever it was that that was.

You are smiling in the picture—
that is always a mistake—
ever so forever and ever it seems.
Your smile brings back no memory
nor touches any loss though
your picture is here before me now
underfoot. Yet I think of poor you,
for so well as I can recall
you forgot ever to ask for mine.

ECHOS

Her arrival in Brooklyn in summer,
not long after the executions of the Rosenbergs
and the McCarthy Hearings, is greeted
with the smell of exhaust and too many people,
the taste bitter in her mouth. She learns
her mother faked her birthplace
on the visa, too terrified to whisper
Soviet Union. The bright sun of home vanishes.

The cardinal's red shines in the trees
of her aunt's cramped yard and signals:
Live and let live, a sentiment her father lives by
not her mother who after too many losses turns
to ancestral sayings aimed to improve
her daughter and all things,
their rhyme lost in translation.

Fin oiven putz, fin hinten schmutz,
(On the outside shine, on the inside dirt)
echoes all these years later when she scrubs,
the glow never enough. Sometimes, the cardinal
appears, sings his song in the front bushes.

JUST TWO SUMMERS AGO
for Dorrie

You sat here on the porch, contained,
the sun hiding behind a cloud,
an enigmatic smile hiding volumes.

You brought with you a new man,
friendship flowering into something more.
He charmed us with his enthusiasms,

his unruly white hair and his blue, blue eyes,
using the time I wanted to spend with you.
You, whose wonder about people
drew them out in momentary surprise.

You, whose world grew larger
encompassing strangers and continents.
You were capable of anything.

Did you know you were dying?
was that the look in your eyes, as he chatted,
a turn inward, our world no longer the thing,

or were you just listening to pain
that persisted through the time
I didn't get to see you?

I did see him again, later.
He was with someone else,
ebullient as ever, blue eyes,
white hair blowing wild.

THE SUN WAS SHINING

Funny you should choose today, under a cerulean sky, to
remind me of Jaffa,
where the sun kept shining and shining and old men
squatted on floor mats
outside ancient stores, *nargilla* hoses in mouths, wares
overflowing
into streets with water sluicing down trenches.

And I, book bag in my hand, daydreamed my way home from
school
through the Arab quarter, my mother's worried face
greeting me,
relieved when I crossed the threshold.

I ran out into sun-drenched sand, a slab of dark bread with
home-made cheese
in my grasp, her voice calling me back. The sun was shining
when she told me
we were leaving, painting vivid scenes of snow-covered
trees, mittened hands,
frosted breath in crisp air. She relived her remembered
youth for me.

I wanted to believe her then but the sun's brilliant glare,
its dazzling shimmer
off shining rocks, the pounding blast of a *chamsin's* heat
stopped my breath
with its velvety asphalt scent.

Soon enough, I looked in vain for sun-burnished ancient
stones, a girl walking,
old Arabs settling into days of waiting, the air hot with
anticipation.

Peter Morrison

MATHILDE

My mind is a theater with many stages
And different corridors leading to each,
On every one a different scene,
Half-played.

I choose the one that leads to you, Mathilde,
When you were a century old,
German-American mother-of-my-friend.
Sit beside me on the living room sofa,
I want to ask you about your life,
Here and over there.
Instead you inquire about mine.

My parents, my sibling, my profession.
Then you excuse yourself so you might feed us,
Where the kitchen table eyes the counter
And dares us to walk between, pull out a chair.

Your son, savoring your sauerbraten,
Speaks in German.
I pick up words: "Hast du...? Wenn ich die Zeit habe..."
My summer of German lessons inadequate.

Three years of lunches prior to each show,
Always different, always savory,
Always as kind as the woman who prepares them.
Only three years...then, "...sans teeth, sans eyes, sans
Taste, sans...everything."

I did not see the final scene,
When you, at 104,
Were glad to be excused,
To receive longevity's everlasting meal,

Prepared *for* you.

George H. Northrup

FOUND: INTO PLOWSHARES
Isaiah 2:4

The Plowshares activists easily cut through
Kitsap's perimeter fence, hiked around
the huge base for four hours,
ignored all the warning signs,
cut through two more fences,
and got to within about forty feet
of where the nuclear warheads are stored.

Father Bix was eighty-one at the time.
Sister Anne was eighty-three.
Father Bix brought along his nitroglycerine tablets
and paused to take some during the long hike.

About twenty marines with automatic weapons
stopped the activists, put hoods on them
to prevent them from seeing any more
of the top-secret facility,
and made them lie on the ground
while the base was searched for other intruders.

When someone later said, "Please, Father,
don't get into any more trouble,"
he laughed and replied, "We're all in trouble."

[Slightly abridged from "Break-in at Y-12," by Eric
Schlosser, *The New Yorker*, March 9, 2015, p. 55.]

IN THE ELEMENTS

Each of the seven falls
on his annual hike
plunges fulsome as ever
despite the recent drought.

Footsteps, aimless and therefore never lost,
bring him by unknown design
to consider the fork of this elm,
the stubs of fallen pine branches,
charred remains of lightning strikes—
each detail joining the careful context
in wordless intimation.

How can this be shared?
He waits for an answer,
sitting on moss-covered rock,
gift of a receding glacier long ago.

Barbara Novack

OUTSIDE THE ABANDONED HOUSE

is a dying tree.
In spring there was life,
laughter in the house.
Now all is cold and empty.
Love is war.
Life is not.

is an untended garden
gray and overgrown with weeds,
all the flowers of springtime
just a memory,
life's melody half-heard
and love's misremembered.

is a swing set
rusted in the seasons since
someone loved a child here.
Then armies opened the garden gate
and strode its grasses
and left devastation
in their wake.

THE WIND-UP WATCH

The batteries have died
the gears have frozen
the workings got wet –
the newer watches sit
in the dresser drawer
in a sad tangle
of untold time.

I retrieve from the back
the old wind-up watch
abandoned for the newer
that need no attention
that run on their own,
effortless blithe beings
that tell time carelessly
tossing off the seconds
minutes, hours
mindlessly
as if they did not matter,
tossing them, like
confetti, in the air.

The wind-up watch takes effort
to find the time each morning
point the hands
and whir the wheel to its
limit.
The wind-up watch has
boundaries.
Its time is finite.

I thought I would resent
its time taking mine
but instead I find it
a meditation
each morning
on the limits
on the value
of time.

MOVING ON

These are the arms I held out to you again and again
These are the legs I opened as a peace offering after we
fought
These are the eyes I shut too many time to count
These are the cheeks I turned and turned and turned

And these are hands that are open and ringless
And these are the legs that are walking out the door
And these are the eyes that see beyond the fog of pain
And these are the cheeks that are dry as this page

And these are the lines I write, my line in the sand
These words are my declaration of independence
These are for the ones that know where I stand
And these are the very last thoughts of you

SOME THINGS WE CAN NEVER HAVE

Across the sea of faces your eyes lock mine for two, three,
four heartbeats,
the intensity of them corkscrewing their way into me.
I turn away, alarmed by my thoughts.

I think of our hello, your voice; heated honey.
My hand had slipped so smoothly into yours as we kissed
cheeks.
Scent of aftershave & perfume lingered in the air.

As the poet read about her mother dying and staying with
the body I cried.
I dared not look up to see what you were doing.
Over one hundred people in the room and all I could think
about was you.

At least I have a new muse for a while, but a few new
poems
don't take the place of a lover's hands & mouth & mount.
To swirl my tongue in heated honey would be much more
fulfilling.

Some things we can never have, one of them for me is you.

WEARING MY FREAK

I put on my 1st layer of freak,
back years ago, when I was
mama's sweet baby girl.

Except mama didn't bother to stay.
Then papa stole all my sugar away.

My alarm clock was his footsteps in the hall.

Love = pain
Books = escape
Foster = home

Unfamiliar car in the drive
tells me I'm going for another ride.

Spin the wheel, see where I stop.
Caseworker cheerfully chats
with my new set of mom & pop.

New school, new group of girls
looking to kick my butt.

Double digits roll around
and papa, they say, is cured.

Pack me up, send me home.
I pile the layers on
so I won't feel the blows.

I'm stuck here in madness,
trapped with no place to go.

Drugging and drinking are my
new best friends.

The abyss grows deeper,
the crap never ends.

Man, the system has plenty of pens
but no balls.
They don't have the vision
to see through my flimsy walls.

They don't have the will, the skill
to stop the beating, the repeating of
his-story.

Stoic is my style,
stoned is my state.

I start wearing my freak very loud,
become a juvenile delinquent,
anything but proud.

No act outrageous enough,
no message gets through.
I just can't tell them, the system,
the dead-in-the-heads at school.

14 brings ovaries enough to bounce,
and the L.I.E. is my jump-off place.
I use my thumb and my smile for the
get out of state, great escape race.

New York to Florida,
damn what a trip.
To club Nowheresville,
I have full membership.

I take as many mini-vacations as I can --
they come in whites, reds, blacks.
Pop one in, sit back, relax.

Waitressing pays the bills
and smokin' dulls the head.
Instead of living numb and dumb
I would rather be dead.

All these layers of freak
are wearing me down.

Therapist
The rapist.
It's all in the spacing.

I'll take door #1 Monty,
let's see what we'll find.

Tearing layers off one at a time,
lightens my load helps free my mind.

I have built a new world,
my destiny is mine.
After all the storms
the skies are clear
for the sun and stars to shine.

But, still, I wear my freak,
on the inside, way, way down deep.
Where a throwaway girl still seeks
a safe place to hide
a safe place to sleep.

Megan O'Keeffe

THE GIVE AND TAKE

In the dark, it is easy to mistake
fantasy for truth. Him for you.
His touch mistakenly tender
like pale poppy petals.
Like the ones I put by your gravestone
this May to remind you
I still think of our 'I do's seven years ago.

But the light hazes in this boundless bedroom
and all I see is clingy, itchy ivy
entrapping my wrist like regret imprisons my thoughts.
I can't take back this one night but still
I pinch my eyes closed again
back to the darkness.

Back when a dark-haired man seemed
like a good idea. Back when
I felt brave and confident
to go up to a man and take
what I desired.

Like when I took from you,
warmth from your chest during the winter nights
and your solitude when watching Sunday Football.
You took from me too,
my half of the covers with all your tossing and turning
and the hatred inside me that grew just like our stillborn.

I took that hatred back though
when you were lowered six feet down.
It's been so long since I've felt your familiar warmth
But I went looking for you in all the wrong places.
You're not in his bed sheets
nor under that tombstone on the ground.

A LOSS OF PROCESS

There is nothing,
a void in the expanses of my aching brain,
no transport of clever ideas,
no strobe lights pulsing pretty colors,
substance absent, capacity reduced,
serenity failing, the peace broken,
anarchy, in a rambling, chaotic micro world,
looking not seeing, hearing no meanings,
no revelations to communicate,
appreciation of beauty removed,
love and joy abstract notions written in invisible ink,
a dingy tile room lit in gray,
defecation aroma, rotten sparkles flying.

I have acute laryngitis,
thought process raw and hoarse.
There is a frog in my mind,
disrupting the cells,
belching the most horrid noises,
a reflection from my mirror,
of a disfigured, deformed, dilated heart,
suffering from a personality crisis,
rooted deeply in past regressions,
swarming over me like desperate bees,
a knife wound reminding,
that it needs dressing, medicine to heal,
cleansing water, pure, cool,
refreshing my spirit, soothing the process,
filling the cavity.

I AM THE LAKE

When the lines are cast,
calling the scaly critters, submerged,
I am living above the world,
free from tension, wringing me like a rag,
breathing freely, worries non-existent.

When the catch is landed,
unhooking under blue ceiling,
releasing the fish, angle a success,
I watch it swim back home,
longing to follow,
for another day's encounter,
a needed brush with nature.

When the wind blows folding the water,
I am the lake, I become liquid,
I lap the shoreline, cradle the fowl,
light and free, unified, organic,
I am a haven for myself.

Rhonda Richmond

A WILLING LESSON

Mother never left me a willing lesson. She always taught me from side roads on busy intersections on the hard side of town, and even then I loved her. She sought the easy way, but never found it. She was bitterness, reflected in the hard steel beams of the stop light that never turned green for our car. Mother loved Mary Jane, Jimmy Bean and old Saint Ives, and still I loved her. I loved her with each hit, each drink, each day she never came back to claim me. I loved her. I always will. Mother never left me a willing lesson, but she left me lessons I never will forget.

POUNDS

Dear Lyn H-E-J-I-N-I-A-N I thought of you the other day
as I watched the six hundred, ninety pound woman speak
her life on the television set. Crying she was no longer
woman.   No longer lady   No longer human.   As
Maybelline flipped the Christi image in the two minuet
breaks. *Am I a woman? Practicing startling*
     accessible? natural in flow and perception?
          She logged her life in fat curls which bleed over to
consume her husband's former rest spot.   I counted my life
in the ever increasing sags that plagued my breasts   in
deep dark multiplying freckles on my back.   But it was
raining.   My hands frozen – freezing – cramped! No pen could
take all the mind could give.   I'm pressing on.
Pressing like the thin girls thighs working the Thigh
Master.   Pumping   pumping   pumping out
     the old image in with the new.   While six hundred
pound lady becomes   515 pound lady   439 pound lady
     364 pound lady   I hug my three pound fat curl
claiming "I am the fat image of my former self!" Gotta
make a change   gotta make a change. Lyn, my image
is burned   has burned out the socket of my eyes.

No pen can write it.

THE RACE
IN MEMORIAM of an abandoned relationship
1971-2008: COLORADO

IN the throes of a sour black night,
buttermilk thick fog straggles

each newly butchered breath,
that twitched its way noisily

up and out of her gullet.
Panting like wild dogs

as it caught pace with the rustling
leaves under her footsteps.

Breasting one child while
towing another,

she scurried toward the unknown;
bitterly clawing away from the familiar.

The past falling like a thick wool blanket
over the dying corpse of complacent regret:

regret that so brilliantly consumed--
all those left behind - - like maggots.

Running to the mysterious unknown
terrified, eager - - afraid. Running!

Ruth Sabath Rosenthal

ABOVE MY GRASSY BED

a butterfly
perches on a daisy
sunshine pierces
wing scrim of amber
squints my eyes
lulls me to slumber
beating beating things
raise my heartbeat
I rouse
butterfly off
somewhere
in its stead
a buzzing bee
prompting me
off my grassy bed
I head home
musing where
that'll be
years to come
and just where
the fancy free
creature is
in its metamorphosis

AT A LOSS FOR WORDS

dad

your coma doesn't stop you
from pacing your touch
like a metronome
thumb sweeping back
and forth on the side
of my hand on the mattress
of your hospital bed
i sit beside
& somewhere the hands
of a clock stop

mom

dad died but
i'm here
like he would
have hoped
now
i'll care for you
think speak
for you mom
blink if you can
remember
me

cousin

She called and said:
He's Dead! Gone
Just like that!

I hung up the phone,
reached for *my* husband,
hugged him hard and long.

GRANDFATHER

How like your wife
my mother looked,
like your wife
felt your love
chill to the bone.

How like your wife
Mother felt
your slam to the face,
your wife not there
to take *those* whacks.

How early in life
your wife dead,
rheumatic fever
you said, though
rumored *your* doing.

Oh, that your wife
would have lived
to know her daughter
married a gentle man,
a decent man.

How I wish that
grandmother of mine,
had been there
to mother more
so I could have.

I REMEMBER THE ZINNIAS

Autumnal hues with bee-magnet centers.
In the planting, seeds of satisfaction
pearled Mother's cheeks with perspiration,
made her glow head to toe. Every year,
zinnias fringed the pathway to our back door
by the kitchen.

Mother loved her zinnias, color-rich, profound
contrast to the dusty-rose brocade loveseat
and sofa, aqua cut-velvet of Father's chair—
each bound in clear-plastic fitted slipcovers
that, in summer, made the backs of our thighs
stick to our seats.

When her new dining set arrived, Mother, keen
it remain pristine, moved Lucky, my beloved
canary, from dining room to kitchen, to roost
inches from pot roasts simmering, fruit ripening,
a window nearby, rarely open. And, child I was,
I didn't protest on my bird's behalf.

Weeks later, just home from school,
I learned that Lucky had died
and Mother had given his cage away.
She claimed to have buried him
(in her tomato patch) just feet
from her prized zinnias.

LOST IN THE FOREST

In a forest thick
With the smell
Of hot blood
A wolf sniffs out
His next victim

Whys echo
Night lifts
Its cloak
& I crawl out
Of bed soaked

In a nightmare
Sweating out
Yet another
Bloody awful
Relationship

LOST DALMATIAN

After the Dalmatian got lost, he decided to find his way home. This wasn't easy, because he couldn't read maps, ask for directions, or recite his name and address for the authorities. He could not even convince the dog catchers that he was not a stray, he was not rabid, he was just a little disoriented after all that dog nip. He'd eaten a few mouthfuls, then passed out and gone home. But what he'd thought was a doghouse had turned out to be a cattle car. There he was, mingling with the herd, trying to blend in, but trying not to end up in the meatpacking yards. Blending in was possible, because he was black and white, like a Holstein. But beyond that, he stood out like a sore hound. So he scooted, with legs and paws flying, and ears and tail flapping, into the wind, away from the smell of doomed cowhide and toward the scent that reminded him of home.

OPHIDIAN DREAM

When the apple tree spread its branches,
a serpent slithered into a forbidden place
nakedness exposed
original sin evoked
and spread across seas accosting souls.

It was only when a Riverman appeared
to immerse mankind in the mouth of the Dead Sea
that there was a cure.
I asked, was I cured, Mother?
Yes, sprinkled with blessed water at St Monica's,

similar to today, as we bathe to cleanse our bodies.
But time is sliding away, Mother.
I'm beyond middle age, now,
tired of paddling in the purling of polluted lakes.
Something has happened.

We live in a world where the serpent is a power cord
and our children are its plug, shocked with no known cure.
Sometimes I wake in the middle of the night
from inexhaustibly running between the moon & sun,
my face pressed against the window of dreams

looking for you . . . looking for you to wink,
acknowledge the vision of an auspicious future.

PEACHES

Oh, how the ladies spring to their heels
awaiting flip-flop days, short shorts,
halters; any way to expose the skin
for required golden summer make-overs.

The heat arrives to cover the island,
open gates for sun worshippers to swarm
beaches, greeted by water's welcomed wave;
and men will follow, some flexing

muscles, most in dark glasses to shadow
conspicuous exercise of the eyes.
I find myself swimming in a minority
pool. Heat just makes me cranky.

In summer, I favor fruit as it ripens
to its finest flavor, to stand in front
of an outdoor market amidst the variety,
to pick and choose by the feel of the squeeze;

and my favorite is the peach.
I peel back its skin to the naked touch,
soak it in juice of the vine,
absorb the sweetness.

Soon, next season will arrive,
the cover-up of bare essential enjoyment,
peaches too hard to squeeze,
memories cast into windblasts.

The taste of fruitful love
vanishes in days of frigid freeze.

SHADOWS OF EMPTINESS

If I lost my voice, I could
still talk with God, ask why
and He would hear those same words
that fall empty on your ears.

If my eyes went blank
to an inside world, black & white,
I'd find a raised wordpad,
carve a cane from an oak tree branch.

If I lost my limbs
I'd still have heart.
If the well runs dry
I'd fill it with dreams.

Maybe, for you . . .
the moon would talk,
the stars would wink.

But if I lost my mind,
there'd be no more imagination.

TRAILBLAZER
in memory of Maxwell Wheat

Whispers in the cool Gazebo breeze
claimed he was at the end of the line.
In all the years I've known him
there was never an end of line
not followed by images wrapped in fresh language.

He not only woke to the warbler's song,
he wallowed through murky footsteps of war
and the spirit of his poems
would make poets and plovers dance.

June 2016, he tipped his wide-brimmed
straw hat to fading faces one last time
leaving lines to keep the beat with nature's refrain,
not to leave grieving followers to starve
beneath the pine boughs, heavy with tears.

As memorial petals begin to bow
and wither into a passing wind,
the efflorescence of new voices
blossoms from his fadeless inspiration.

Steven Sher

WRITING HER NAME ON THE LABELS OF HER CLOTHES

Although we write her name in black
on every label and elastic band,
sometimes nightgowns
or white socks once washed
wind up with someone else.

When misnamed items
find their way inside her drawers,
she picks them out and puts them on,
greeting us with silence
in strange clothes we've never seen.

One day we'll come and find the lobby
strewn with scraps of memory
from her long life, other residents
rummaging through them, discovering
something colorful to wear to lunch.

And all we thought was permanent,
written on our hearts in her once exquisite
script, will start to fade.

Nathan Singer

SUGAR....OR SHINE LIKE THE SCAR

Are you lost again, little magpie?
Should I play the 'possum or should I
catch you when you fall?
Do what you gotta do,
whatever you gotta do,
and I'll come get you when it's over.
And I'll hold you 'til you can sleep again
and I'll swallow the disease.

Go ahead, Sugar.
Be who you gotta be
with whomever you gotta be.
Sweating and squealing siamese.
Dance in the waters, I'll sleep in the weeds.
Be a friend when you need a strong back.
And I'll keep it back
I'm pressing back the darkness.
So cut me and I'll run and bleed elsewhere.
It's just the skin
and the bones
and the innocent toxic joy
It's my day and a half
left content and alone
and you're sore
in your joy
in your glory.
Now fade and rot.
Savor the dull ache and the desire for less.
And less still?

And less still.

Our love is thick and absolute
like wet down in my lungs.
Our love is forever,
endless,
eternal,
like the whisper in my left ear
and the ringing in my right.
Our love is solid and secure,
pressing down and back.
I am Sisyphus AND Atlas
encumbered by bliss.
I consume your love
familiar yet consistent—
pepper, lemon, clove, ash,
and I am a Roman on holiday.
Your love consumes me.
I reach heavenward for the warmth
the heat
the passion.
And I am a cripple in La Brea.
Yeah, your love sticks,
lingering. . .seeping. . .
And I can stand up straight
just to be beaten down again
or I can lie still
sinking in the tar forever.

Did you touch hands and leave me sick there?
Leave me their sick when they're sick?
Taken out by the scorpion or your poison tail.

And the disease presses back
as I'm swallowing your darkness.
Our love is green, Sugar.
Like hiding in the bay window shrubs.
Our love is blue, Sugar.
Like Coltrane on a rainy October night.
Our love is red, Sugar.
Like a fist into cinderblock.
Our love is brown sugar, or
moist earth over a fresh grave.

Ask, "why don't you love me?"
Ask, "why do you make me hurt you?"
Say my only way out is right through you.

You crawl back to me scarred,
bashed,
      beaten
           bloody,
                bruised,
                    used,
                        abused,
                            refused,
                                choked,
strangled, mangled, tangled, teased,
                          twisted,
                    tricked,
                pricked,
            dicked,
        kicked,
belt-licked,
sugar-sick,

diseased,
infected, subjected, and
rejected. . .
But. . .
you'll always be my baby, right?
You'll always be my baby.
And the only way out is right through me.
Twisted,
tricked,
pricked,
belt-licked,
sugar-sick,
and your only way out is right through me.

And I can stand up straight just to be beaten down again
or I can lie still sinking in the tar forever.
And I can stand up straight just to be beaten down again
or I can lie still
sinking in the tar forever.
And I can stand up straight
just to be beaten down again or I can lie still sinking
in the tar forever.
And I can stand up
straight
just to be beaten down again or I can lie
still sinking in the tar forever.
And I can stand up straight
just to be beaten down again
or I can lie
still sinking
in the tar
forever.

Hal Sirowitz

MY DEAD HAMSTER

My parents bought me a hamster,
but our cat thought the present was
for him. I kept the hamster in a cage
to keep him safe from harm. But
the cat would not be stopped. He'd
kept staring at the hamster, intimidating
him. One day, I found the hamster dead.
His heart stopped beating. Fear must
have killed him. Mother said this was
a good lesson. Hate can kill. Therefore,
I wasn't allowed to hate my sister,
no matter what she did to me. I couldn't
even hate myself. From that moment on,
hate wasn't allowed to linger in the house
or in the front yard. Stomping
wasn't good for the grass.

George Snedeker

FATHER

My father was born in 1899,
Two years after a Great Depression,
In the shadow of the poorhouse.

When he was five years old,
His two-year-old sister drowned
While following a duck into a pond.
He had only wished that she would go away.

FURNITURE OF THE WORLD

The garbage bags that lie in the streets
Give my eyes
something to hold on to.
Without concrete objects like these,
I'd be lost.
We all need a floor to stand on
And the furniture of the world.

HELP

The art of life can no longer be seen.
Our ears are filled with more than wax.
I cannot hear what you are trying to say,
No matter how hard I try.

LONGING

Two bodies gripped in passion,
In a night of sanity
Until the madness returns

In the morning,
When a simple embrace
Is all they desire.

LOST

In dreams
I am often lost
On the wrong subway or bus
Headed in the wrong direction
Surrounded by strangers.

Ed Stever

SIDEWALK RESURRECTION

Outside on the sidewalk
a man in a blue
checkered shirt
smokes a Lucky,
gazes down at the concrete curb
that fronts the dialysis center.

He flicks the butt into the gutter
and pivots toward the building,
where he is swallowed
in a cave of darkness.

Douglas G. Sweezy

#1460 (COSMOS)

Under a canopy
Of lazy afternoon sun
On a June afternoon
Tearing out the infestation
Separating soul from stain
Seed from disdain
Leaving the wet soil
To nourish the stalks
Of sunflowers, cosmos and larkspurs
An exercise in purging
Sometimes the breath of breadth
Is centering
And during the purge
Parsing the dirt
Enduring memory:
Harvesting a hot pink heel
Solo
Belonging once to a Barbie or Skipper
Left behind after a wild
Bender one night
Or running to catch the train
When the strap broke
And left it to board
Or be faced with waiting
Hours for the 4 A.M. drunk car
Full of oafish belligerency

Was it a remnant of
My wife's childhood?
One from our niece?

The plastic piece
Found its way now
To the wooden window sill
Above the kitchen sink
To soak
Up the sunlight
Colour of thought
Fading

Erstwhile

In a mix of movement
Rearrangement of furniture
Rooms
Lives
Separating out
Memory from thought
Planets from the sun
Moon from the stars
Thick blankets from thin sheets
Wiry yarns from wicker baskets
Across the ceramic floor
A shimmer of silver
A stich marker
A moment in time
A tiny ring with a clear
Iridescent bead glimmering

This, too, to the sill
Beside the shoe
A bracelet for Barbie
She wore once

To one of her hallowed
Rock shows
Lost to the groupies backstage
Or for the most important
Business meeting to impress
The investors
And burnish strong ties
For the success of the
Company name

But really
What is of import
Is not the object
- The things themselves -
Not even the memory
- These were not my toys -
But their promise
The imagination they help
To incur, deliver
As now the cell phone rings
And it just might be Ken
Calling to let me know
The jet is fueled up
And ready to go

Patti Tana

THE COMFORT OF NEAR THINGS

I'm halfway through the second night
of three that you're away.

Stepping out of bed, I feel you
rise and follow me to the window
to peer out into the dark.

Numbers on the cable box stay the same
no matter how many times
I squint at them.

The dog is stretched out
on your side of the bed
resting her head on your pillow.

Back in bed, I turn my pillow over
and sink my cheek into the soft cool cloth.

HOW I FOUND OUT

when I open the door
he's leaning back in a chair
she's kneeling before him

my hands grip the doorframe
to keep me from falling

so that's how it is
I say to myself in the silence

a door is an exit
as well as an entrance

SEISMIC SHIFT

You know how it feels when you're stopped
in a car, and from the edge of your eye
you see the car next to you move?

Hands clutch the wheel
foot slams the brake
as your brain recalibrates what's real.

That's how I feel now.

A moment ago I stood on solid ground.
Now sand slips beneath my feet
as the tide recedes from the shore.

JR Turek

POEM FOUND FROM THE LOST

I've lost my keys and found them,
lost my wallet and panicked until I found it,
lost one earring of a pair several times
several different pair, and found one earring
makes a great pendant.

I've lost weight and found it,
lost dogs and found them,
lost my patience, my sense of humor
and self-control but never lost
my wedding band or my husband's trust.

I've lost old dreams and found new ones
I'd rather pursue, lost memories
and some of them are better gone,
lost my mind but it's too young
to travel too far.

I've lost family and friends
some forever, some to meet again
(in hopes) in heaven.
I've never lost my faith
and pray I never will.

I've lost knowledge but not the thirst
for learning, lost recklessness and found
a stable way to live, lost algebraic formulas
that I never used and won't go looking
to find.

I've lost my hat and found a cold,
lost a dollar and found a penny, lost a bill I forgot
to pay and it cost me more than just money,
lost new poems and found old ones,
lost old poems and found new ones.

I've lost experience but never the lesson,
lost my hold on nicotine, lost more socks
than an elementary school could use,
lost careers and jobs, money and bets,
found new strains of life in the back of my fridge.

I've lost what I thought was everything
and found that I still had more than some,
lost things I can't remember but
will always regret,
lost pens and great ideas forever.

I've lost my way but eventually found it
figurative and metaphoric,
lost my truck in a parking lot
and eventually found it,
lost the habit of freaking out
about minor things
but never lost my ulcer,
lost hope
and found it in a friend's arms.

POSTHUMOUSLY YOURS
to Marilyn

I can remember a time without you,
see my wedding photos that you're not in,
no wedding party gown, no reception dance,
no toast to the future and I remember
not knowing you then, regretting missing you
before we met for more than 32 years.

Two weeks after we wed, we met you
through Paul's business associate,
someone we stopped associating with
several years ago but no need to go into that —
you know the story, the one that ends
not-so-happily after a black eye
and you stayed with us for a fun summer
while you found a new place to live.

After Friday night dog school,
we'd come over for pizza, Keebler just
a puppy then, gone now since 2008,
would try to eat pizza through your glass-
topped dining room table and every week
I'd Windex away his drool and you'd smile,
marvel at how we went from no dogs
to four in short order and you laughed,

and years later, you bought a house,
the house that calls to me to drive past
at least once a week, the vacant one
for sale as-is, with windows cataract-blind

and doors bolted closed to keep the secrets in,
the one without a welcome mat,
but if I sit there long enough, I can hear
the faint echo of chlorine laughter,
mouth salivating with barbeque parties
and dogs barking, cavorting, swimming
– eternal summer you and me memories.
I remind you how you would laugh at us
having four dogs and we both laugh, look at
our four and your four, and cocktails in hand,
break out into schoolgirl giggles.

Christmases and Easter dinners, birthdays
with your mom, my parents and brother, smiles
and jokes, nothing better than family and friends
and great company always with dogs everywhere.

Now, jumping far ahead I know, you left two
and we have two left and so many things
remind me of you and it hurts like breathing
with a stake cleaving my heart to pieces.
So many connections, it's eerie,
like you were 62 and I'm 55,
and you were born in 55 and I was born in 62,
and the only quarter I found in that house
was from 1962, and lottery tickets, losers all,
totaling $62, and I can barely go on,
remembering how I'd call you some midnight
just knowing that something was wrong
and you not even surprised by my knowing,
our 'spidey-sense' as we called it, one more
connection and then...   nothing.

No return calls to mine, no email replies
and then the call that you were in a coma
and we were there every day until your eyes
fluttered open, and I spent four days in that house
scrubbing up after dogs left alone too long,
did hours of laundry between carpet steaming
and tile cleaning and something happened,
something snapped cracked popped. It was different,
you were never the same, never responded to the pleas
as Godmother to our dogs to come for a visit, stop by
once in a while, call/write/email, but you didn't,
even when we lost Snapple and four months later
lost Hershey...   and nothing.
We never knew how bad it got, how deep you were
in places we couldn't get to or get you out of,
even lending you thousands of dollars
we'll never get back couldn't do it... but we didn't know.

A Thursday in November, a call from someone
we don't know tells us you're gone. Just like that.
Two detectives found you passed out in a gas station
cigarette burning in the ashtray while they rushed you
to the hospital but it was too late. Just like that.
Fingers snap in my head, a connection sizzles,
dies, and we're left wondering why we have
so many questions, no answers.
We've lost you, lost you long before we realized
but I will keep our you-and-me memories alive,
will think of you every time I see a Dalmatian anything,
a flamingo, a woman hiding a black eye, even pizza,
and you'll live on long beyond the pain of now.

LOOKING BACK AT 2019

February 11th, my brother's birthday, I get a letter, "Congratulations! You have been selected to be the 2019 Long Island Poet of the Year by Walt Whitman Association." I am honored, surprised, proud, all things at once. I bring the letter to show Mikey, *Look, and the letter is dated for your birthday, too!* His response is "Oh, that's nice." He's not into poetry so his lack of enthusiasm is ok. I am still delighted.

On May 11th, Paul and my 34th anniversary, another surprise. I am awarded a first place in the PPA 23rd Annual Poetry Contest. I show Mikey the framed certificate and the check... He doesn't always show his emotions, and I'm good with that.

Summer comes and brings another fabulous surprise – I win the Newsday Garden Poetry Contest. Sunday after church at Mikey's, Paul opens *Newsday* and smiling and chuckling brings the paper with the photo, article, and my poem into the den where Mikey and I are watching tv. *Wow!* from me, "That's cool" from Mikey. I'm not hurt or disappointed.

Then the PPA Haiku Contest first place and again I bring the certificate and check to show Mikey. "Hey, yeah, good for you." I've known him 57 years; that's his way.

Finally, late summer, I am honored with the title of Superintendent of Poetry for the LI Fair. I am amazed and dazed with excitement. I bring Mikey the news and get the reaction I expect. It's all good.

I tell you these things not out of bragging – that's not me at all – but because they converge at a point I never ever expected. Fast forward, I find out in October, at Mikey's wake, that each time I brought him an award, a newspaper article about something I was doing or being honored for, the next day, he went into school where he worked and told everyone from teachers to administration to the principal "Hey, look at this! This is my sister, the poet!" And weeks later, I find every newspaper article two and three times, all the copies of letters and awards I brought him, all of it in piles in his room and throughout the house, lovingly saved.

I am glad to know he was proud of me, even if he couldn't show me but told the world just the same. What neither of us knew was that my new poetry book, *Midnight on the Eve of Never*, would be delivered to my publisher on the day of Mikey's funeral. Without him saying it,

I know he's wild with pride. Thanks, Mikey – love you lots!

*   *   *

keepsake
heart-shaped trinket box
holding treasures
you once held

(Senryu)

PHOTO ALBUMS

for Michael M. Raffaele
February 11, 1961 ~ October 19, 2019

A relic from the past, snapshots held in place
on a black page with white corners you needed
to lick and stick in place. Page after page
of posed people with toothy smiles beside
landmarks and loved ones preserved on
slick squares, a distinct odor permeating
each photo.

Color, black and white, sepia browns
that yellow, all adhered to stay in place
to preserve the moment. The advent
of white pages covered with a film
you pulled back and placed photos
to a slightly sticky page and replaced
the clear film, or pages with a pocket
you slip the memory into. I find a history
of all of these, Mikey, in your shelves
of albums. The lick-and-stick augmented
by double-sided tape that will outlast
a nuclear explosion, and those pockets
that sealed smiling faces melted to adhere
memories like glue to a clear window.

Those pull-and-stick pages don't stick well
and a landscape of panoramas puddle
at my feet in release. I wanted to pick and
choose which of the hundreds of snapshots
I would keep and integrate into my own
burgeoning collection of albums, but time
refused to comply with my wishes, like

wishing you and I could sit on the couch
today, an album open covering our legs,
pointing and laughing at antics captured
for eternity, but now eternity is all I have.
You've gone on to a place where glue
doesn't matter, where sticky messes
never happen, where your memories
are written in ripples of clouds every morning
and night. I collect my favorite photos,
snap them into my cell phone and carry you
with me stuck to the walls of my heart forever.

Muriel Harris Weinstein

LOST

"It just couldn't be worse!
I lost my baby today.
Where's my baby?

If I don't find him who will feed him?
Who will diaper him?
If I don't find him, I'll cut out my tongue."

Momma sobs,
throws herself across the bed.
I throw my arms around her.
"Momma dear, your baby, Steve, is gone.

He left when he was twenty-nine
Momma, that's over thirty years ago.

Remember the hospital sent him home?
It was painful to care for him
You called, said you needed my help.

Remember Dr. Keriensky's words,
"Steve's body's poisoning him."

I say it slowly,
enunciate with a sharp edge
so my words can cut the spidery threads
tangled in her memory.

"I wasn't watching him carefully.
He's so beautiful, everyone wants him.
They want to touch his red hair.

I know he was stolen. I know it.
I left him in the baby carriage.
Mybaby, mybaby, how can I live?"

ODE TO LOST POEMS

I lost the poem I wrote
about a lost poem I found
I wrote it late last night
and now before dawn,
its words stabbing my sleep,

I rise to finish it
but it has flown.
Now there are two lost poems.

If I write another about loss
will that follow the others?
Is there a Valley of Lost Poems
where they yearn to go?
If I prevent them from leaving,
by using permanent marker
or sneak them into the freezer
and read them with gloves on
will they stay or will they sigh
like crying winds
and rebel by printing in faded ink
planning in dawn's early light take flight
anyway.

I think I'll corral all lost poems
make a safe haven
where they'll form their own colony.
Before reading I'd ask, would you like
my voice sotto voce, basso or alto
would you want a trio in the background

or be read by the fireplace?
If you like outdoor breezes ruffling your paper
I'll stand under a willow where even the birds will hear.
But with all these promises
do you think they'll stay?
I have a hunch they'll find a way
to slink away.

Charles Peter Watson

INSTAGRAM POST
(for the record)

When I saw a discarded cassette tape
laying in the street, I reminisced and asked,
'Will we still speak through ink and paper
beyond the reaches of the digital age
or leave their reign back among the cassette tapes,
the phonographs, UHF, the 8-track, the telegraphs, et al,
as Edisonian winds blow across that graveyard?'

We once told of lost times of our life in the paleolithosphere
but extinct tongues unrecorded died in transit
to leave the word of mouth a long lost, abandoned trail.
The telegraph predates Morse, even town criers.
Guttenberg wasn't Zuckerberg but greased the same
skids,
Who owns the state of the art?
When will the art be the artifact?
It's in your hands now.

Marq Wells

THIS BOY

Trapped within a bone dry and brittle exoskeleton,
I trudge the streets of the old neighborhood,

in order to find a younger more resilient cycle of myself
to slide   back into.

After an eternity, I finally discover the crumbling abode
where by now the elements have dislodged
most of the white shingles
and sheets of gray plywood
overlap shattered window panes.

I venture behind this once vibrant home,
pushing my way through mutant weeds,
spider webs, twisting vines,
into some crackling shellacked land where
the sun sticks fast to one spot in the sky
and a young boy of about nine
sits cross-legged in a sandbox.

With haunting blue eyes,
he lifts his gaze to meet mine
while he gloats over miniature graves
swollen with insects that
bristle and writhe just below
the slightly shifting surface sand.
And the boy asks:
            Don't I know you from somewhere?

And we both recall what Mother said
about all those kids who lived right across town,
their flat grey faces smiling up at us
from the sides of milk cartons and posters
pasted up in five and dimes and every other
telephone pole across town.

And after another moment,
this Boy's lips stretch in a primordial grin
as we listen to all the insects
that haven't been collected yet
screech in an obscene choir high in the tree tops overhead,
oblivious to this boy and his intent or
their   imminent implacable   end.

FOUND POEM

rolled up
inserted in a bottle
seven prisoners, ages 18-20
names, camp numbers, hometowns
Auschwitz
Sept. 9, 1944

construction crew
Oswiecim, Poland
discovers bottle in concrete wall
April 20, 2009

POEM FOUND

65 years later
erev Yom Hashoah
(day before
        Holocaust Remembrance Day)
silenced   screams
        evidence
                testify...
May their souls rest in peace.

LILACS AND MOTHER'S DAY

wave to me from neighbor's yards
hang out over stranger's fences
cluster at neglected curbsides.

Lilac—Mother's favorite flower
once tied by childhood hands
into fragrant bunches
wrapped with purple grosgrain ribbon
welcomed by her eyes delighted.

I try to grow my own
lime the earth, prune back old canes
raise my hopes with heart-shaped leaves
but no bud is gifted me—
no blossom to stir memory.

Instead, I reach for metaphor
to explain the dearth of bloom
offer meaning, reasons why—
find my peace with dreamer's dreams
lilacs in a lilac sky...

                *   *   *

One more year—my calendaring
since Mother's Day
last year's seasonal lament:
no lilacs lush and lavender
to remind me of bouquets once picked
bunched and bundled—grosgrain ribboned
given amid giggles, smiles...

This year, I must confess, I barely glance

see my backyard bush bloom green—
let it be, just let it be
until my husband points out to me
one purple cone
        backlit by sun
              waiting   waiting   waiting...
        Mother's gift to me.

WHEEL OF FORTUNE
as you would desire yours to be respected... --Sayings of the Fathers

Within the trove of trivia,
goals and guides to ethical life,
abide the cautions—precautions
for treasures
        Lost & Found

Should one lose a thing unique,
such salient news
description—inscription,
probable place of misplacement
best be posted
in a prominent space
or widely read local ledger.

Should an item found be deemed generic
or of indeterminate merit—
a coin, a comb,
cheese likely to rot,
it is not incumbent
to search—research
the apparently absent "lostee."

But, should said item be
identifiably of worth,
the finder must
industriously seek
the owner or point of origin—
register an ad, consult a listing
resisting immediate need and greed

for the greater good
of what he or she would ultimately desire to transpire
if himself the one less fortunate
until time and trial—
quest and denial
establish beyond doubt
that what once was lost is now found
and officially, ethically, may be claimed.
Case Closed!

Acknowledgements

Sybil Bank:
I CANNOT FIND
originally published in *River Over Stones,* 2014

SWEDASAI – LITHUANIA – 2004
originally published in *Performance Poets Ass   Vol 15*

TRANSITIONS 1996- A TRIPTYCH
originally published in *River Over Stones,* 2014

Amy Barone:
PICKING UP THE PIECES
originally published in *The Brownstown Poets* anthology

UNFINISHED
originally published in *We Became Summer* (NYQ Books)

Carol Barrett:
HOME MOVIE
originally published in the author's collection *Calling in the Bones* (Ashland Poetry Press,) 2005

IMPELLED TOWARD LIGHT
originally published in *Earth's Daughters,* 1989

LARKSPUR TRAIL
originally published in *Crosswinds Poetry Journal,* 2016

Peter Thabit Jones:
LESSON
originally published in 'Garden of Clouds/New and Selected Poems' by Peter Thabit Jones (Cross-Cultural Communications, 2020)

POETRY READING, THE ROBERT FROST FARM
originally published in 'Garden of Clouds/New and Selected
Poems' by Peter Thabit Jones (Cross-Cultural
Communications, 2020)

Norbert Krapf:
INDIANAPOLIS ELEGY
originally published in *The Indianapolis Review*

HOLDING ON AND LETTING GO
originally published in *The Tipton Poetry Journal*

THE RETURN OF SUNSHINE
originally published in (ACTA Publications, 2018)

Neil Leadbeater:
LEAVING NEW STREET
originally published in *Quarry* in 2009

Maria Manobianco:
BEST SAID PLANS
originally published in the Bards Annual 2018- A Poetry
Anthology

ROCK OF AGES
originally published in the PPA Literary Review Vol. VI

Barbara Novack:
OUTSIDE THE ABANDONED HOUSE
originally published in *Dancing on the Rim of Light* published
by Blue Light Press (2020)

THE WIND-UP WATCH
originally published in *Dancing on the Rim of Light* published
by Blue Light Press (2020)

217

Steven Sher:
WRITING HER NAME ON THE LABELS OF HER
CLOTHES
originally published in *Long Island Sounds 2019*

Nathan Singer:
SUGAR. . . .OR SHINE LIKE THE SCAR
originally published in *The Journal of Kentucky Studies* vol.
20, September 2003

JR Turek:
POEM FOUND FROM LOST
originally published *Midnight on the Eve of Never*, JR
Turek; 2109, Words With Wings Press

POSTHUMOUSLY YOURS
originally published *Midnight on the Eve of Never*, JR
Turek; 2109, Words With Wings Press